www.brookscole.com

www.brookscole.com is the World Wide Web site for Brooks/Cole and is your direct source to dozens of online resources.

At *www.brookscole.com* you can find out about supplements, demonstration software, and student resources. You can also send email to many of our authors and preview new publications and exciting new technologies.

www.brookscole.com
Changing the way the world learns®

Clinical Supervision

What to Do

and

How to Do It

ROBERT I. COHEN

Australia • Canada • Mexico • Singapore • Spain
United Kingdom • United States

THOMSON

BROOKS/COLE

Executive Editor, Helping Professions: Lisa Gebo
Assistant Editor: Alma Dea Michelena
Editorial Assistant: Sheila Walsh
Technology Project Manager: Barry Connolly
Marketing Manager: Caroline Concilla
Marketing Assistant: Mary Ho
Advertising Project Manager: Tami Strang
Signing Representative: Rodger Klas
Project Manager, Editorial Production:
  Jennie Redwitz

Print/Media Buyer: Jessica Reed
Permissions Editor: Kiely Sexton
Production Service: Mary Grivetti, Shepherd, Inc.
Copy Editor: Patterson Lamb
Cover Designer: Cheryl Carrington
Cover Image: Getty Images
Compositor: Shepherd, Inc.
Text and Cover Printer: Webcom

For more information about our products, contact us at:
Thomson Learning Academic Resource Center
1-800-423-0563
For permission to use material from this text, contact us by:
Phone: 1-800-730-2214
Fax: 1-800-730-2215
Web: http://www.thomsonrights.com

Library of Congress Control Number:
2003106293

ISBN: 0-534-63027-8

Brooks/Cole—Thomson Learning
10 Davis Drive
Belmont, CA 94002
USA

Asia
Thomson Learning
5 Shenton Way #01-01
UIC Building
Singapore 068808

Australia/New Zealand
Thomson Learning
102 Dodds Street
Southbank, Victoria 3006
Australia

Canada
Nelson
1120 Birchmount Road
Toronto, Ontario M1K 5G4
Canada

Europe/Middle East/Africa
Thomson Learning
High Holborn House
50/51 Bedford Row
London WC1R 4LR
United Kingdom

Latin America
Thomson Learning
Seneca, 53
Colonia Polanco
11560 Mexico D.F.
Mexico

Spain/Portugal
Paraninfo
Calle/Magallanes, 25
28015 Madrid, Spain

Contents

Preface

I began writing this book 30 years ago. I had just received a call from my adviser in graduate school, asking me to supervise a first-year master's of social work student. I was so flattered. I was so petrified. Why me? I had just gotten my own degree. Isn't it a bit soon? She essentially told me that even though I didn't know what I didn't know, *she did* and she would supervise me (as she had done for my clinical work) from start to finish.

I had already been a supervision junkie as a counselor at the University Counseling Center at SUNY, Stony Brook, getting several hours a week of individual and group supervision for myself. It was what beginning therapists did in those days if you wanted to provide "good" care before managed care, or what I now call managed profits. If truth be told, it was also a way to deal with the terror of possibly hurting someone. I checked with my posse of supervisors. They pretty much agreed that taking the next step would be a "growthful" experience for me. They were the grown-ups here; who was I to disagree? I took the assignment, and ever since, I have been writing this book.

To be more precise, I have been writing this book in my head. Like most people, I prefer order over chaos and as a beginning clinician and supervisor, I often felt the chaos of my inexperience and lack of knowledge. Studying and applying practical conceptual frameworks while doing clinical work and supervision has always been a calming and grounding activity for me. Over time as a professor, supervisor, and trainer, it seems I have been able to help "reduce the noise" for others as well, by helping them bring some order to their work. Without fully realizing it, my research, clinical work, supervisors, supervisees, students, and colleagues had been helping me shape this book in my head into a book in print.

The major goal of this book is to provide a clear and straightforward framework for thinking about and doing clinical supervision. Lum (2000) describes a framework as a "structure that systematically arranges parts of a whole, so that an observer can understand the relationships of components to each other. It is a mosaic or a puzzle that has been completed for the viewer to behold" (p. 114). The framework that is offered here organizes the components of the supervisory process and is intended to provide a coherent picture for the experienced and inexperienced supervisor alike "to behold." It familiarizes the newer supervisor or graduate student with the "language" of supervision in a format that is comprehensive, relatively simple to understand, and practical to use. Veteran supervisors are reminded of what they already know, yet are given a new mosaic to which they can attach their experience and systematically apply future learning.

The book is informed empirically and theoretically, but does not pretend to do in-depth analyses of supervision or an extensive review of the literature. There are many sources available that do and the reader is referred to them throughout the book. If used as a core text for courses in supervision, the book provides an organizing schema that can simply be enriched in breadth and depth with assignments from the existing literature. At the same time, it is comprehensive enough to stand alone and may easily be used for training seminars and continuing education.

The book makes liberal use of examples and case illustrations that come from my clinical practice and experiences as a supervisor, professor, consultant, and trainer. The case material is intended to make the more didactic features of the framework come alive for students and practitioners alike. Many examples get into the heads of the supervisor and supervisee and provide a unique feel for the concepts illustrated. (The names and exact configuration of the facts have been deliberately changed to protect the identity of the participants.)

The case illustrations come from situations across the helping professions. My own training and academic degrees are in clinical psychology and social work; however, I teach and learn from people in counseling, marriage and family practice, alcohol and drug counseling, nursing, pastoral care, and psychiatry. The principles discussed in the text are consistent with their best practices and are generally applicable to the supervisory standards in these professions.

The organization of this book provides a process phase framework for thinking about and doing clinical supervision that takes the reader from engagement in the first three chapters through to the work phase in the last four chapters. The engagement phase is a time when the supervisee is oriented to the process and structure of supervision and a time most critical to the development of a safe and trusting relationship—the foundation on which the rest of the supervisory work is built. The work phase builds on engagement and focuses on the supervisee's direct work with clients. Assessments are effected, and supervisor and supervisee collaborate to create goals for growth, action plans, and criteria for success. Finally, supervisors intervene to facilitate professional growth and if they have administrative responsibility, manage the fit between the needs of the agency and the needs of the supervisee/staff member.

During discussion of the engagement phase in Part I, clinical supervision is defined, roles are specified, and the initial supervisory contract is explained as a dynamic agreement that spells out mutual expectations, goals, and responsibilities. In addition, the process and structure of individual and group supervision is described as orientation continues and then transitions into the work phase. Success in the engagement phase often depends on the supervisor's core relationship-building skills, cultural competence, and ethical use of self, and these skills and attributes are highlighted and illustrated in the three chapters that make up Part I.

Supervisors continue to use these skills in the work phase, of course, as the focus shifts more directly to the supervisees' clinical work with clients. Discussion in Part II begins with assessment. Supervisors use direct and indirect methods to discover specific information about supervisees' problems and strengths as they work with clients. This information is understood in a context that is guided by the supervisees' multicultural attributes, experience, development level, and learning style. As problems and strengths are assessed, feedback is regularly provided and summarized in the formative assessment. Supervisor and supervisee collaborate to determine goals for growth based on findings from the assessment, and they create action plans with criteria for success in order to build on strengths and remediate problems.

Discussion of the work phase is completed as intervention possibilities are explored first from the perspective of the supervisor's clinical role as a facilitator of professional growth. These possibilities center on educational, empowerment, and culturally competent interventions. Interventions are then discussed from the perspective of the supervisor's administrative role as a manager. In this role, supervisors are responsible for risk management including legal and ethical implications as well as the formal evaluation process that is part of the supervisor's gatekeeping role. Supervisor/managers also have the responsibility to negotiate the "fit" between the needs of the agency and the needs of the supervisee/staff member; the use of a basic win/win intervention strategy is discussed in this regard.

As the reader follows the organization of the text, it may appear at first blush that the features of the engagement phase and the work phase neatly follow each other over time in the phases described. Please rest assured that they don't—at least, not as neatly as one would like. Supervisors, for example, are *always* using their relationship skills to develop safer and more trusting interactions with their supervisees (from engagement right through the work phase). They are *continually* assessing their supervisees' skills and attributes as they gain experience and expertise over time and *regularly* evaluate before, during, and after every intervention. And, in fact, it could be said that intervention occurs from the first interaction of the supervisory pair to the very last!

Such is the problem when describing each component part of a mosaic. One can observe and analyze each tile individually, for example, but the mosaic itself makes sense only when one zooms back to see the configuration in its entirety. Conveying a clear picture of the supervision framework offered here by describing each of its component parts may present a similar difficulty. Writing, by necessity, is a linear process, and although the organization of the chapters provides a generally logical sequence to the phases of clinical supervision, the components are just not *perfectly* sequential in real life. This is a short book. Read it twice.

ACKNOWLEDGMENTS

I would first like to acknowledge the students, supervisees, and workshop participants I have worked with for the last 30 years whose wisdom and strengths have taught me most about doing supervision. I particularly want to thank my psychology colleagues and students at SUNY, Stony Brook, and the University of Rhode Island and social work colleagues and students at the Rhode Island College School of Social Work and the Stony Brook School of Social Welfare. Thanks, too, to my partners at Management Support Services and Boston University's Corporate Management Education Center who urged me to "cross over," learn about management, and teach and coach in business settings. (I'm hopeful that the social and health service managers and administrators I work with have been helped by virtue of "crossing back.")

I have facilitated a number of ongoing supervision groups in my private practice, two of which have been running continuously for over 20 years, and several in agency settings that have been going for almost as long. What staying power you all have, and what dedication to your clients and your learning!

Thank you in particular to the Wednesday and Thursday groups; Erin Minior and the staff at JFS; Brother Mike Reiss, Rob Archer, and the staff at Tides Family Service; Father Bob Rochon and ten years of class with C.P.E. students; Eileen Dunleavy and the staff at FRFS and St. Vincent's; Joe Hyde at the Drug and Alcohol Training Association of RI; Ellie Collins and Jim Wilsey and the psycosocial oncology group leaders at Roger Williams Medical Center; and Skip Granai, Amanda Goldstein, and the staff of the Women's Oncology Program and Breast Health Center at Women and Infants Hospital.

I also want to acknowledge my supervisors at Stony Brook: Francis Brisbane, Gerald Green, Erna Kaplan, Esther Marcus, Dave McWhirter, Doris Silverberg, and K. Dan O'Leary; and at the University of Rhode Island, James O. Prochaska, my major professor in the psychology department. Thank you, Jim, for your support when I was writing my doctoral dissertation and for telling your inspiring stories about the peaks and valleys you experienced writing your first book. Such differences in style and approach you all have! I thank you for the common thread in your work, the ability to help me discover the best parts of who I could be with the people I work with and help.

I am most grateful to my good friends and colleagues who have not only been forthcoming with their intellect, but have been generous with their care and personal regard for me. As usual, my oldest friend Peter Balsam was able to reframe the toughest moments of this project into an adventure. (Where did an experimental psychologist who works with animals get such skill?) Donald Koch, Rick Reamer, Craig Scott, Nick Tishler, and Allison Curley were particularly helpful and supportive in getting this project going and getting it finished. Special thanks also go to Daisy Broudy, Nate and Sue Chernov, Donna Palumbo, Barry Plummer, Joan Ray, Deborah Siegel, Rick Soloman, Martha Straus, and Diane Thompson for their ongoing interest and support. And of course, my men's support group of 24 years, Bob, Bobby, Donald, Francis, Jim, John, Steve, and Tom, are owed a special debt of gratitude for keeping me honest, grounded, and sane.

I wish to give special thanks to Lisa Gebo, my editor, whose ability to analyze and manage a complicated start can only be rivaled by her support in helping to create a successful finish. Thanks too to editorial assistant Sheila Walsh, who was "there" at every step of the way. I would like to thank Jennie Redwitz, Mary Grivetti, and Patterson Lamb, as well as reviewers Angeline Barretta-Herman, University of St. Thomas; David Fauri, Virginia Commonwealth University; Patricia Polanski, University of Dayton; Frank Weathers, Auburn University; and Geoffrey Yager, University of Cincinnati.

Above all, I want to acknowledge the love and support of my family. Thanks go to my parents, Artie and Estelle (now deceased), who taught me the value of persistence and hard work (indispensable in this book-writing business, so I have learned). My sister, Dorothy Cohen Fleischer, has always been my anchor and "biggest fan." I want to thank her for who she is to all who know her, and in her capacity as a clinical social worker, I want to thank her for all the free consultation she has given me over the years. To Tom, from whom I am given the affectionate title "parental unit," I want to thank you for being my computer consultant, for taking time out (along with your buddies) to give me breaks from writing, and for being a great son. Last but not least, I dedicate this book to my wife, Sue, for your daily love, constant support and sacrifice, and four years of study dates together.

Robert I. Cohen, MSW, Ph.D.

PART I

⚜

The Engagement Phase

Constructing a Foundation

The early stages of the engagement phase of supervision, the point at which supervisors orient their supervisees to the structure and process of supervision, are described in Chapter 1. Supervisors define supervision, introduce their supervisees to their respective roles and functions through role induction, and outline an organizing framework for supervision such as the one suggested in this book. In addition, the supervisor initiates the supervisory contract, which specifies clinical and administrative responsibilities, learning objectives, action plans, and criteria for success: a kind of mutual job description. (Over time, supervisors and supervisees review the initial supervisory contract and periodically make revisions.)

During this period of orientation and engagement, supervisors also work to develop safe and trusting relationships, the focus for Chapter 2. To do this they evidence core relationship-building skills, cultural competence, and the ethical use of self. The core skills that are reviewed here include a supportive presence, psychological and physical attending, listening, empathy, challenging, and self-management. Supervisors also effectively relate to their multicultural supervisees (and they with their clients) using culturally competent contact and engagement skills. We focus on these in a context based on the examination of several basic models and approaches, highlighting Lum's (2000) practice process stages as well as a method used for ethnographic interviewing.

Chapter 2 concludes with a review of common ethical standards that govern professional behavior across the helping professions. We review such principles as informed consent, due process, confidentiality, multiple or dual roles and relationships, and appropriate boundary decisions. We end by examining the ethical use of power and ethical caring, constructs that are particularly compelling for the supervisory relationship. The core skills, cultural competence, and ethics are discussed throughout the organizing framework as they impact the supervisory relationship in both the engagement and work phases.

Chapter 3 reviews the individual and group formats for supervision, which completes discussion of the engagement phase. Each format provides a somewhat different forum to effect each of the components of the supervisory process as supervisors and supervisees move into the work phase. Supervisors explain the process and structure of each as explicated in the chapter. The chapter also discusses several kinds of groups in the clinical setting, necessary steps in the preparation of a group, stages of group development, and a comparison of the advantages and disadvantages of each approach.

We begin discussion of the engagement phase next.

1

⚜

Beginning
the Supervision

This chapter starts by defining clinical supervision. Next is a description of role induction as discussed during orientation, followed by an overview of the initial supervisory contract. As supervisors negotiate the supervisory contract with their supervisees in the engagement phase, they *simultaneously* evidence certain attributes and utilize certain skills that help the development of the supervisory relationship and specify the structure and process of the individual and group supervision formats. These are reviewed in Chapters 2 and 3, respectively.

CLINICAL SUPERVISION DEFINED

Clinical supervision is a process whereby a person in a supervisory role facilitates the professional growth of one or more designated supervisees to help them attain knowledge, improve their skills, and strengthen their professional attitudes and values as they provide clinical services to their clients.

Clinical services refers to such direct services as counseling, psychotherapy, and case management that supervisees provide to individuals, couples, families, or small groups. This basic definition of clinical supervision assumes that supervisors work to create a safe and trusting supportive relationship with their supervisees so that the supervisees can work effectively. It also assumes that clinical supervisors, at minimum, monitor the quality of their supervisees' work on behalf of their clients to ensure sound practice according to professional ethical standards and the laws of the land.

The definition may be modified to include additional roles and functions that depend on the setting in which the supervision occurs. Clinical supervisors in agency settings, for example, generally assume administrative functions such as monitoring and evaluating the quality of the supervisee's work according to the policies and procedures of the agency. They also often manage the fit between the needs of the agency and the needs of their supervisees (as staff members), even if they are not formally designated managers. Supervisors are also frequently in gatekeeping roles for accrediting bodies such as graduate schools or professional training institutes or for the state as they monitor the supervisee's work for the purposes of certification and/or licensing.

Our definition may also be applied differentially, depending on the context and contract for mutual service. For example, the supervisory work may vary depending on the experience and developmental level of the supervisee. Supervisors who agree to work with student interns or newer supervisees will "facilitate professional growth" in ways that may be quite different from their interactions with experienced clinicians seeking an occasional supervisory consultation around a difficult case. The context and contract for clinicians doing peer supervision or consultation with each other will be different still; however, in this and all cases, the basic process of clinical supervision is essentially the same: to facilitate professional growth (equated here with attaining knowledge, improving clinical skills, and strengthening professional attitudes and values) with the assumption that the quality of service provided to clients receiving clinical services will be appropriately monitored.

As supervisors prepare to meet and orient prospective supervisees, they must have a clear understanding of the processes and structure that organize the work of clinical supervision. (One of their responsibilities is to outline this process and structure for the supervisee.) These guiding principles parallel the organization of this book; in the pages that follow, we more fully develop this organizing framework. As the framework unfolds, consider the following question as a central point of orientation:

> Given the nature of our relationship (and the level of trust and safety that develops), and what I know about this supervisee (based on my ongoing assessment), how do I intervene (which interventions should I choose to 'facilitate the supervisee's professional growth' and 'administratively account for the needs of the agency and staff') in ways that help the supervisee reach the learning objectives and goals for growth we have agreed to (in the supervisory contract) and that ultimately best serve clients?

Notice that the orienting question includes the reference to "*administratively account for the needs of the agency and the staff*." We focus mainly on ongoing supervisory relationships in this book where there is an expectation that the supervisor has an administrative role in an institutional setting and is accountable to the needs of the agency and staff. The term *agency* is used in the book for simplicity, with the understanding that clinicians from the helping professions work in other institutional settings as well, such as hospitals, prisons, places of worship, and schools. The basic definition offered here assumes that the clinical supervisor monitors the quality of service to clients according to legal and professional standards; however, we highlight consideration of these features when we discuss the contract later in the chapter and managerial interventions in Chapter 6. Thus, in this chapter, monitoring functions of the supervisor are related to administration in the agency setting.

ROLE INDUCTION: ORIENTING
THE SUPERVISEE

When supervisors begin the engagement phase and meet with their supervisees, they orient them to their respective roles: *who* they are to each other as they begin their journey together. They also orient them to a framework of supervision such as the one organized in this book: *what* they will be doing and *how* they will be doing it together. This orientation is essentially a process that is referred to as role induction (after Fischer, 1978). During role induction, the roles, functions, and framework of supervision are outlined as a cognitive road map that orients the travelers to the supervisory landscape. The actual trip for every supervisory pair will be different, depending on a host of variables, but as the supervisor explains to the supervisee, they mostly fulfill functions that depend on the needs of the client, the supervisee, the agency, the profession, the law, and the supervisor (albeit from different angles!).

When orienting the supervisee to roles and functions, the supervisor explains that supervisors have two main roles, which follow from our discussion of the definition of clinical supervision and the orienting question for this book. The first role, associated mainly with the clinical definition of supervision, is "facilitator of professional growth" and relates to supporting the supervisee's learning needs for knowledge, skills, and professional attitudes and values. The second role, concerned mainly with administration, is "manager"; it relates to accounting for the needs of the agency vis-à-vis the staff, and extends to the gatekeeping needs of the profession and the law. Both of these roles and the functions associated with them are *always* involved with attending to the needs of clients—now and in the future.

Haynes, Corey, and Moulton (2003, pp. 21–28) summarized the literature and compiled a comprehensive list of supervisory roles. The list is adapted here to describe the aforementioned clinical and administrative roles in terms of supervisory functions. Education and empowerment are the two main functions that relate to the clinical role of facilitating the supervisee's professional growth. Teaching, advising, mentoring, consulting, coaching, and acting as a sounding board are functions included under the rubric of education. Strength-based approaches represent functions included under empowerment. Certain features of the core helping skills have both education and empowerment functions. To be sure, the clinical supervisor, who functions as a supportive, yet sometimes challenging role model, wears many hats!

When supervisors also assume the role of manager, an administrative role that focuses mainly on accounting for the needs of the agency and staff, the list of supervisory functions is expanded. It includes several administrative functions such as helping to carry out the mission of the agency on behalf of clients while ensuring proper risk management (e.g., attention to legal and ethical issues, and evaluation). It also involves managing the "fit" between the agency's needs (e.g., monitoring, interpretation and implementation of policies and procedures) and the supervisee/staff member's needs in response. This middle management role often requires good negotiation skills to help facilitate this fit. We define and discuss these functions more fully in Chapter 7.

Orienting discussions regarding the supervisees' roles generally cast the supervisees as *clinicians* (or *service providers*), *learners,* and *staff members.* In their roles as clinicians, their major function is to provide clinical services to clients appropriate to the requirements of their job responsibilities and the scope of their abilities. As learners, their main function is to grow professionally in their clinical roles by engaging in activities that will help them attain knowledge and strengthen their skills and professional attitudes and values. As staff members who work in an agency setting under the auspices of their chosen profession and the laws of the land, they have administrative functions that relate to the fulfillment of agency policies and utilization of resources in good faith and with a spirit of cooperation. They also often seek to advance their professional careers through graduate training, and certification and licensing, and they frequently seek the support of the supervisor and agency to aid in the credentialing process.

(Staff members who are clinicians in agency settings receiving peer supervision may also be considered "learners" to the extent that they request and receive supervision from peers. Also, students doing field internships are considered to be service providers and staff members—for the purposes of this book—as they function administratively in the agency in many of the same ways as regular staff, with expectations to perform within the standards of their chosen profession and the law. Of course, the expectations for their service are modified to fit the needs of the supervisee, clients, agency, and sponsoring institution.)

As mentioned in the preface, the framework we discuss in this book is applicable *across the helping professions* and is appropriate for supervisees (and supervisors) at all levels in their development. The case examples and illustrations used throughout the book more or less reflect this. Our first case example involves a student who comes from social work. Sam, a second year student/intern, meets with Dave, his supervisor, for their first "orientation" meeting.

It's Sam's first day in his social work field placement. Dave, his supervisor, remembers being nervous during all of his "first days" (even going back to kindergarten!), and he plans to make this first meeting as safe and comfortable as possible. He welcomes Sam to the agency and shows him the space he will be sharing with another student.

Dave says that the agenda (sometimes called session goals) for this first meeting is to tell Sam a little about the agency, and explain the framework for supervision, his role as supervisor, and Sam's role as student/ intern. It's a time to start getting to know each other and Dave is interested in learning about Sam's experience and level of development. He briefly explains the kinds of services the agency provides and how services are delivered; he assures Sam that it will probably take him some time to put it all together, although he facetiously adds that "there'll be a test at the end of the day."

Sam appears relatively self-assured, even for a second-year student, and Dave reminds himself how important it is not to project his nervousness onto Sam. Dave tells him that he will have the opportunity to work with individuals, couples, families, and groups as well as do some family life education. He explains that his job is to get to know Sam and to provide a safe atmosphere where Sam can risk being fully forthcoming about his practice and learning needs. Dave asks Sam to tell him if anything gets in the way of that safety. Dave assures him that they will meet regularly and review his work to provide him with feedback that Sam can use to increase his knowledge, improve his clinical skills, and strengthen his professional attitudes and values—and of course, to monitor the welfare of his clients.

Realizing that he has been doing most of the talking, Dave switches to listening mode. He asks Sam about his previous experience and if he knows what he wants to get from this experience. He assures him that it "isn't a requirement to know exactly at this time" and that they will be talking about his interests and learning needs regularly as time goes on. (Dave knows that beginning clinicians and students don't always have the words or concepts to describe what they want from supervision and what they want to learn.) The rudimentary steps to assessment have begun!

Dave listens and listens some more. He notices a genuineness about this young man that he likes and realizes that they are both more relaxed than they were an hour ago. At the same time, Dave starts to feel a bit antsy. Their time is just about up for today and he hasn't yet discussed the specifics of the supervisory contract, the methods he uses to make assessments and evaluations, a number of administrative procedures and legal issues, the formats for supervision sessions and how he likes to organize time in those sessions, and so on. Dave thinks to himself, cool your jets! We're just starting. Let's not overwhelm this guy in his first hour here. Shake the man's hand and tell him we've got more to talk about next time. He did just that.

◁▷◁▷◁▷◁▷◁▷

Ideally, supervisors want to orient their new supervisees as completely and quickly as possible to the framework for supervision, their roles, and the learning objectives and responsibilities of their contract. At the same time, they know how important it is to carefully build trust and safety during this engagement phase. Figuring out how to pace these complementary processes can be a challenge even for experienced supervisors, such as Dave, given the sheer volume of information to be covered and the disparity in experience, level of development, skills, and attributes among supervisees as well as the needs of clients, the agency, and/or the profession. For more information about roles and functions for both supervisors and supervisees, the reader is directed to the following: Bernard and Goodyear (1998), Haynes et al. (2003), Holloway (1995), Kadushin and Harkness (2002), Kaiser (1997), and Munson (2002).

Having discussed a beginning orientation to roles, functions, and the structure and process of supervision, we focus next on the supervisory contract. This is used to specify clinical and administrative responsibilities, learning objectives, action plans, and criteria for success.

THE SUPERVISORY CONTRACT

As a continuing feature of the orientation, the supervisor introduces the initial supervisory contract. This contract is a dynamic agreement between the supervisor and the supervisee that spells out mutual expectations, responsibilities, and requirements and serves as a kind of mutual "informed consent." Additional reasons for having a contract are well documented. Falvey (2002, pp. 37–54) summarizes the literature and discusses the nature and benefits of the contract at length. She concludes that contracts "help prevent miscommunication, facilitate orientation of the supervisee, minimize covert agendas and abuses of supervisory power, and reduce the legal exposure of all parties" (p. 42).

The content of supervisory contracts can look quite different for different combinations of supervisors and supervisees. Factors like the supervisee's level of development, experience, multicultural attributes, and learning style; needs of the clients, the agency, the profession, the law, and the supervisor—all can affect the content of the contract. The supervisory contract is dynamic. It is continually modified over time as trusting relationships develop, more complete assessments emerge, or growth occurs because of successful intervention related to the supervisee's problems and strengths. Contracts also change to reflect changes in practice settings or the credentialing needs of the supervisee.

Therefore, when supervisors discuss the supervisory contract with their supervisees during orientation, they present it as an initial contract and in so doing also fulfill the ethical responsibility for informed consent. The initial contract becomes an ongoing supervisory contract that is reviewed periodically. The structure of the contract, however, should remain constant and should contain some standard features—responsibilities and criteria for success, for example—that correlate to the supervisee's roles as *clinician, learner, and staff member* and the supervisor's clinical role as *facilitator of professional growth* and administrative role as *manager.* We discuss first those features of the supervisory contract that are related to the supervisee's roles.

Supervisee's Role as Clinician

The contract delineates the supervisee's clinical responsibilities as well as criteria for success (criteria that tell both supervisor and supervisee that responsibilities have been satisfactorily achieved). Clinical responsibilities are those tasks and activities that generally satisfy expectations for service with clients. Listed below are responsibilities generic to the clinical role:

- Develop safe and trusting clinical relationships. This activity focuses on the supervisee's responsibility to use core relationship-building skills and to demonstrate cultural competence and ethical use of self (according to the ethical standards of the professions and the laws of the land).

- Orient clients to the process and structure of clinical work through role induction and the clinical contract. This involves clarifying for and with clients each person's role and responsibility in doing the clinical work and ways that clinical meetings are structured and processed.

- Do thorough assessments that account for client problems and strengths and are conceptualized using sound theoretical and empirical approaches. Assessments include methods that are appropriate to the particular needs of the client and consideration of multicultural attributes and other features that suggest intervention modalities appropriate to the change process (perhaps, for example, through the use of—but not limited to—formal diagnoses based on the *Diagnostic and Statistical Manual of Mental Disorders,* 4th ed., or *DSM-IV-TR* [American Psychiatric Association, 2000]).

- Set well-formed goals and criteria for success. In collaboration with the client, decide what goals are desirable for change based on the assessment and criteria for success.

- Choose and utilize appropriate interventions that are based on the assessment and goals and that reflect best practices and professional standards.

- Evaluate progress periodically and renegotiate the clinical contract as needed.

Notice how these features of clinical work mirror the process and structure of supervision as presented in this book. Similar to most clinicians, supervisors build trust and safety in developing relationships using core skills, cultural competence, and ethical use of self. They also do role induction and negotiate contracts and discuss the structure and process of meetings as well as assess for problems and strengths in a context that accounts for multicultural attributes and the particular needs of the client (in the case of supervision this involves experience, developmental level, and learning style). In addition, supervisors (like clinicians) collaborate in setting goals, action plans, and criteria for success based on a sound conceptualization of problems and strengths, intervene in ways that are tied to assessments and goals, and do evaluations.

Clinicians attend to these processes in ways that depend on their theoretical bias or previous training. Although the topography may be different for different clinicians, they usually do some version of this dynamic sequence. Because of the similarities between supervision and clinical work, often the supervisor is, in effect, facilitating the supervisee's professional growth and modeling at the same time. (I call this the *dual process* and refer to these similarities and their implications throughout the text.)

The dual process is to be distinguished from two other similar concepts discussed in the supervision literature: the *parallel process* and the *isomorphic process*. First presented by Eckstein and Wallerstein (1958), the parallel process suggests that behavior exhibited by clients in therapy *may at any one point in time* "parallel" behaviors presented by supervisees to their supervisors. Edwards and Chen (1999, p. 354) review the literature on isomorphism and discuss it in depth as a systems phenomenon where there also is pattern replication similar to the parallel process. The main difference is that with the isomorphic process, a change in one system will correspond to changes in the other system as a normal expectation.

Kaiser (1997, p. 4) suggests that both of these terms are "used to describe a connection" with what actually happens in the treatment situation and the supervisory situation. Whereas these concepts are useful to explain certain dynamics of behavior that occur in supervision and therapy, they are different from the "spirit" of the dual process, which focuses on *conceptual similarities* in process and structure. As we discuss our process phase framework for supervision in this book, it is helpful for the reader to notice ways that supervision and clinical work are similar and how, at times, they differ.

Despite similarities in the conceptual framework for supervisory and clinical work, there are indeed specific features of the actual practice of therapy and supervision that are quite *dissimilar* for supervisors vis-à-vis supervisees and clinicians vis-à-vis clients. Differences relate mainly to *purpose, focus,* and *roles* (after Kadushin & Harkness, 2002, pp. 200–204), and it is ethically important for supervisors to be clear about these distinctions so as to keep strict boundaries between the professional and personal lives of the supervisee.

Kadushin and Harkness make a distinction between facilitating professional growth and personal growth in terms of the differences in purpose. They suggest that the supervisor's

> responsibility is to help the supervisee become a better worker, not
> necessarily a better person. The legitimate concern is with the professional
> activities of the supervisee, but the supervisor has no sanction to intrude
> into the worker's personal life. The concern is with changes in professional
> identity rather than changes in personal identity. The supervisor asks, "How
> can I help you do your work?" rather than "How can I help you?" (p. 200)

The focus and role of the supervisor are also different from those of the clinician. Kadushin and Harkness point out that the focus of the supervisor's role is connected to the "professional growth" of the supervisee and not to personal growth, as it is in the clinical situation. They do not deny that professional growth can have consequences for personal growth, and that the professional self is an important part of the "personal-self configuration." However, they say that should therapeutic change and growth happen, a likely (and often welcome) occurrence, it should be "an incidental, serendipitous, unplanned, unintended by-product of the focus on professional growth" (p. 200).

At the same time, Kadushin and Harkness do acknowledge circumstances when supervisees' personal feelings, behavior, and attitudes may affect the quality of their work and *require* specific supervisory attention. For example, the supervisee may experience a countertransference reaction, or sexual feelings for a client, or "burnout" resulting in impaired behavior. These situations do fall within the purview of the supervisory interaction and must be considered ethically, if not legally. In fact, some in the field suggest that methods to deal with the possibility of such circumstances should be specified up-front in the supervisory contract (Haynes et al., 2003). We discuss the clinical and ethical implications of these issues further in Chapter 6 in the section on "self management skills."

Continuing our discussion of the supervisee's clinical role as stated in the supervisory contract, it is useful to have a clear, initial agreement regarding criteria for success that show satisfactory completion of the supervisee's clinical responsibilities. The contract should have a provision that answers the question, "What will tell us that you (supervisees) have successfully completed your clinical responsibilities?" Specific behavioral criteria that are established early clarify expectations and provide a foundation for later evaluations. These should be included as part of a statement regarding the methods of evaluation, frequency, and due process procedures in the agency if there are major disagreements. (We discuss evaluation methods as part of the supervisor's administrative responsibilities in the contract later in this chapter, in Chapter 5 as part of our discussion of the formative assessment and Chapter 7 in the context of the summative evaluation.) Discussing them up-front in the contract also accomplishes the ethical responsibility to provide for informed consent and supports administrative interventions regarding risk management.

Supervisee's Role as Learner

Discussion about clinical responsibilities and criteria for success transitions well to consideration of the supervisee's learner role in the supervisory contract. That is because learning is a lifelong process, and regardless of experience and level of development, all clinicians have room to strengthen their practice with increased knowledge, improved skills, and a deepened understanding and utilization of professional attitudes and values. To aid in this pursuit, the supervisory contract specifies the supervisee's learning objectives and the action plan necessary to reach their objectives as well as criteria for success.

Supervisors and supervisees talk about learning objectives early in the engagement phase of supervision because as with any journey, it's best to be informed about one's destination prior to actually "leaving the station." Beginning with the end in mind, as Covey (1989) might suggest, supervisors and supervisees consider what outcomes are desirable as "destinations" for their journey together. They then agree on what steps will be taken in order to "guarantee arrival." Finally, they discuss the criteria that would demonstrate that, in fact, they have "arrived successfully."

Several variables can affect how the learning objectives are chosen and when. One variable that can derail this process, for example, is that the supervisory pair may not know enough about each other to make good choices, particularly when they have not had the time to establish a safe and trusting relationship. Experience and developmental level are also important variables. Less experienced workers or students may not know how to conceptualize appropriate learning objectives, much less an action plan and criteria for success. They may need a fair amount of assistance in choosing specific learning "destinations"—a bit like using the service of a sophisticated travel agent.

Sometimes, however, students enter their field placements or internships with predetermined learning objectives that are extremely specific. These may be part of a prepackaged field education or internship curriculum that all students follow. The supervisor has the task in these circumstances to clarify the meaning and implications of this information for students who don't yet have the experience to grasp the material. In cases like this, students have little or no opportunity to have input into their learning goals, at least in the engagement phase of the supervision.

Advanced students or experienced clinicians who are well known to the supervisor, on the other hand, may contract for supervision with very clear and detailed learning objectives in mind. They may have more than rudimentary understandings and skills and can insightfully determine quite specific objectives. For instance, a more experienced supervisee may set as a learning destination to know more about a specific method of intervention—for example, the cognitive/behavioral approach—and learn to apply the skills inherent in this approach with depressed clients.

Learning objectives typically focus on increased clinical knowledge and skills and enlightened professional attitudes and values specific to the processes and structure of clinical practice (such as developing relationships, assessment, case conceptualization and goal setting, and intervention methods). Supervisors also encourage learning objectives that support the supervisees' abilities to "self-supervise." To do that, they must have an understanding of professional role, intra- and interpersonal emotional awareness, and self-evaluation (after Holloway & Acker, cited in Holloway, 1995, p. 13).

As learning objectives become conceptualized and included in the supervisory contract, the supervisee and supervisor decide on the action plan that will be used to reach these goals as well as the criteria for success. The number and kinds of learning objectives are a function of the needs of the supervisee, clients, the agency, the supervisor, the profession (or sponsoring institution), and the prevailing laws. The following are a few typical examples of learning objectives, action plans, and criteria for success:

- *Learning Objective:* Increase knowledge about strength-based interviewing methods
  Action Plan: Read *Interviewing for Solutions,* 2002, by De Jong and Berg
  Criteria for Success: Complete book; make presentation to staff

- *Learning Objective:* Come to supervision meetings prepared to discuss cases
  Action Plan: Conceptualize cases, prepare questions, and have progress notes in order prior to meeting
  Criteria for Success: Demonstrate preparation in meeting by having conceptualized cases before the meeting, asking relevant questions, and producing up-to-date and organized progress notes

Because the supervisory contract reflects a dynamic process between supervisor and supervisee, basic learning objectives over time may no longer be relevant and may be dropped as others are added. They also may be modified or replaced with goals for growth that are determined on the basis of direct feedback, formative assessments, and summative evaluations that pinpoint strengths to build on and/or problems (clinical or administrative) that call for remediation. (We discuss these situations more fully in Chapters 5, 6 and 7.)

Supervisee's Role as Staff Member

In addition to their roles as clinicians or service providers and learners, supervisees have administrative responsibilities that are spelled out in the supervisory contract along with criteria for success. Informed consent in this part of the contract provides an ethical base for the supervisee's understanding with respect to administrative expectations for service. Supervisors specify practical, nuts-and-bolts type responsibilities that satisfy agency policies and procedures, and supervisees are asked to utilize agency resources in good faith and with a spirit of cooperation.

Practical responsibilities to which supervisees typically agree include hours of service and on-call coverage; type and number of clients (as well as other duties such as serving on committees); proper documentation (including commitments to provide statements of confidentiality and informed consent to clients); agreement to follow policies regarding emergencies and other risk management policies that involve ethics and the law; agreement to attain professional certification or licenses as required; and agreement to participate in evaluation procedures.

Kraines (1991, pp. 32–33) refers to such responsibilities as the work contract, completion of which is simply expected. He contrasts this to the psychological contract, which is a bit more subtle and refers to the "music behind the words" or the spirit that accompanies the work. It's the notion that one utilizes the resources of the agency in good faith and goes beyond the letter of the law or contract for the greater good, perhaps to complete a project or help out a fellow worker or manager who is shorthanded. This spirit of cooperation is difficult to specify in any work contract but is often crucial if the supervisee is to be an effective member of a successful work team and staff.

Specific administrative agreements for work responsibilities are tied to behavioral criteria for success, which clarify expectations, reduce the likelihood of miscommunication, and provide a foundation for later evaluations. For example, statements such as "complete and update records by the end of each month," "read and comment on formative assessments every 10 weeks," a n d "arrive on time and prepared for weekly supervision meetings" clearly inform the supervisee of expectations and clarify at the start how to recognize a successful finish. This process enhances Kaiser's (1997) press for "shared meaning" in the developing relationship and most simply, increases the prospect of a harmonious relationship by preventing misunderstanding. Consider the following case example of Jane and her supervisor, Deane, who might have benefited from greater specificity in their supervisory contract.

Jane is the volunteer coordinator and supervisor for a multiservice outreach program in the inner city. When she was hired, her supervisor Deane provided a job description outlining her clinical responsibilities and several administrative responsibilities including biweekly supervision meetings. (The job description serves as a kind of supervisory contract in this context.) Although the program is already well established and mainly requires coordination, there are times when active recruitment is needed; however, this responsibility is not explicitly stated in Jane's supervisory contract. After some months, it becomes apparent that more volunteers are necessary to staff their voter registration drive. Deane offhandedly mentions to Jane that she should "probably begin the process of finding additional volunteers."

Two supervisory meetings go by and neither Jane nor Deane follows up on Deane's comment about recruitment. Six weeks after this assignment is delegated, Deane realizes that there are no new volunteers. Puzzled, she asks Jane in their next meeting about her lack of progress on the recruitment front. Stating that she is overworked and underpaid, Jane defensively explains that she doesn't have time for recruitment and further, "There is nothing specific in my contract that said I had to actively get new volunteers." Although Deane might have been more direct with her statement about the assignment (other than briefly mentioning that she should "probably begin the process . . ."), she believes that recruitment is inherently part of the job.

Was Jane defensive about the task because she got "caught" not doing her job? Was she really feeling quite overwhelmed with her responsibilities and didn't know how to talk about it with Deane? Was she blowing smoke about being overworked so as to avoid dealing with her incomplete assignment? Did she fear cold-calling strangers and asking them to volunteer? Did she not realize that this was part of her job responsibilities?

When Deane actually confronts Jane (skillfully employing the use of "caring confrontation," which we discuss in the next chapter), she learns that there is a grain of truth in each of the reasons mentioned. Jane and Deane work out their difficulties, but they might have had an easier time had they established greater specificity regarding responsibilities and criteria for success earlier in the work contract. Jane's statement that recruiting isn't specified in her written job description and therefore is not required is a good example of a subtle violation of the psychological contract.

Supervisors, like Deane, do well to spell out clinical and administrative responsibilities for and with their supervisees. They too have such responsibilities in their roles as managers and facilitators of professional growth. We turn next to a review of these roles and accompanying responsibilities as they are reflected in the supervisory contract.

Supervisor's Clinical Role as Facilitator
of Professional Growth

A major clinical responsibility of supervisors is to create and maintain a supportive and safe learning environment, their end of the psychological contract. They discuss this with their supervisees as part of the orientation and as a function of their clinical role as facilitator of professional growth. Similarly, supervisors review the other features of the supervision framework as they provide an overview of their own clinical responsibilities included in the contract.

Clinical responsibilities include orienting the supervisees to their roles and functions, outlining the process and structure of the supervision, and discussing and negotiating the contract. They also include the other features discussed in upcoming chapters such as developing the relationship (including attention to cultural competence and ethical use of self); individual and group formats for supervision; use of direct and indirect assessment methods (in a context that accounts for experience, developmental level, multicultural attributes and learning style); evaluating clinical progress; helping to set learning objectives, goals for growth, action plans, and criteria for success; and methods of intervention. All of these clinical responsibilities are geared to facilitate the supervisees' professional growth (knowledge, skills, professional attitudes and values) and the successful accomplishment of their clinical learning objectives, goals for growth, and service to clients.

Supervisor's Administrative Role as Manager

Clinical supervisors also have administrative responsibilities as managers (even if they don't see this as their main role). In addition to being accountable for the needs of the client, they are specifically accountable for the needs of agency, and by extension, the profession they represent and the laws of the land. As such, supervisors should include information in the contract about agency risk management policies (including legal and ethical considerations, evaluation, and documentation) and practical nuts-and-bolts procedures and policies.

They also often represent the needs of their supervisee/staff members and help negotiate a satisfactory fit between their needs and those of the organization (we discuss this more fully in Chapter 7). Sharing information about these administrative responsibilities (as well as the clinical responsibilities discussed above) is important for supervisees' informed consent and should be discussed by supervisors as part of the supervisory contract. We briefly summarize several of these areas below as contained in the supervisory contract and discuss them more fully in Chapter 7 in the section on interventions in the role of the manager.

Because they are legally and ethically responsible for the actions of their supervisees, supervisors monitor all the supervisees' cases, assign only those cases that are within the capabilities of their supervisees and within the limits of their own expertise, and track personal and professional limitations that could affect the quality of the supervisees' work. They review the codes of ethics of the pertinent profession with particular reference to confidentiality and informed consent, abandonment, and boundary considerations such as dual and multiple relationships. Legal issues are also discussed as a matter of informed consent including mandatory reporting laws; standards of care; privileged communication; negligence; and statutory, negligent, vicarious, and direct liability. These features are included in the codes of ethics of most of the helping professions as well as the risk management policies of many agencies (including providing full disclosure about them to the supervisees as part of the supervisory contract).

In addition to ethical and legal considerations, supervisors review practical responsibilities with supervisee/staff members and establish the expectation that they will regularly monitor these features of the work contract. One way that supervisors monitor success in these areas (and demonstrate that they are serious about the supervisory process) is to commit to a schedule of regular uninterrupted individual and/or group supervision sessions. Supervisors keep and disclose that they are keeping records (including progress notes) about these planned supervision sessions as well as procedures for availability in case of emergencies. Supervisors should also disclose the format, the intervals, and the processes by which feedback is given and formal evaluations are conducted (for both the agency and/or outside accrediting bodies), in addition to agency policies regarding due process.

We return now to the case of Sam and Dave who are working their way through the orientation process and the initial supervisory contract— obviously no small task!

Sam is completing his third week of placement and is beginning to get a feel for the agency and his supervisor. Other staff and the administrative assistant are extremely helpful in orienting him to some of the policies and procedures of the agency. He has been shadowing a senior staff member who isn't supervising this year, and she is glad to let Sam sit in on some family therapy sessions and explain the intake and record keeping procedures to him as well as other practical responsibilities. Because she has a special interest in ethics, she works with him on some fundamental concepts such as dual and multiple relationships, confidentiality, informed consent, and mandatory reporting laws. In addition, she reviews some of the practical implications associated with these ethical challenges and the National Association of Social Workers (NASW) code of ethics.

There is plenty to do to get Sam oriented and assess some of his basic skills and attributes. Sam, on the other hand, wants to get started with clients yesterday! Dave is concerned about assigning too few clients to Sam. The agency census is low (as it often is at this time of the year), and he would like to assign more than just one or two cases to start. Dave remembers obsessing about the only two clients he had during the first month of his internship; any shift in the relationship or missed appointment was cause for unnecessary angst. Having several clients at the very beginning actually takes some of the pressure off! Sam is eager to begin the work phase, however, and the next two clients are his.

In the meantime, Dave is getting to know Sam better and coming to understand more about his previous experience, developmental level, and learning style. As a second year student who had had two years of practical experience working with adolescents in a group home before coming to graduate school, Sam has several specific ideas about what he wants to learn. These go beyond the basic, very general learning objectives already outlined for him by the School of Social Work in the prepackaged supervisory contract he must use.

For example, Sam wants to learn more about doing solution-focused family therapy, an approach he received some training in during his group home experience. Dave is delighted (mainly because he knows enough about this approach to be able to teach Sam something about it!), and because, thankfully, it fits in with the agency's trend toward strength-based treatment.

As Sam begins to see more and more clients, the focus for the supervisory sessions will shift more toward assessing his work, setting up goals for growth based on observations of problems and strengths in formative assessments, giving him feedback, and so on. For now, both he and Sam complete an agenda for the next few sessions that further reviews Sam's learning objectives and the responsibilities he will carry out to meet these goals and other administrative responsibilities. (Sam has volunteered, for example, to be the student representative on an agency-wide "service delivery committee.") Dave would like to lock in an initial supervisory contract before Sam gets knee-deep in his work with clients, and he tracks the areas of disclosure he must cover before there is final agreement on the provisions of the contract. They are getting closer. So far, so good.

Whether the contract is highly structured and documented in written form or more loosely organized and negotiated verbally, it must initially reflect agreements about basic learning objectives and clinical and administrative responsibilities. In addition, both the supervisor and the supervisee must have a thorough understanding of the structure and process of supervision as well as the respective roles of the supervisory pair. Such knowledge will greatly facilitate the development of the supervisory relationship.

A number of supervisor skills and attributes are particularly helpful in developing the relationship in the engagement phase. These are considered next. Please remember that the relationship develops *simultaneously* with role induction and negotiation of the initial supervisory contract in the engagement phase (as well as the description of the individual and group formats discussed in Chapter 3). In fact, it is always developing!

2

Ⅶ

Developing
the Relationship

Supervisor Skills and Attributes

Ask the most experienced supervisor, the newest supervisee, and every clinician in between about the importance of a safe and trusting relationship. Each will answer that all helping processes begin with development of that relationship. There is always debate regarding the centrality of "the relationship" in the process of change or growth, but most agree that at minimum, some rapport is a necessary if not sufficient condition for the work to be useful. In this chapter we review several sets of skills and attributes that are used to build rapport and establish a strong foundation for the supervisory relationship. These skills and attributes complement negotiation of the initial supervisory contract and role induction in the engagement phase and description of the individual and group formats for supervision.

Core relationship skills are reviewed first in this regard followed by a discussion of skills and attributes specifically associated with cultural competence in relation to multicultural clients and supervisees. Important components of the ethical use of self in the engagement phase are reviewed in the last section of the chapter. Supervisors facilitate trust and safety as they develop the beginning relationship by using these skills and evidencing these attributes. They continue developing the relationship, of course, in the work phase; however, there is a shift in emphasis at that time to assessment, evaluation, goals for growth, and contract revision and intervention.

CORE RELATIONSHIP SKILLS

Successful clinicians and supervisors alike find ways to build rapport and relate well to their clients and supervisees. This is particularly important in the engagement phase of supervision. A good working relationship provides a necessary foundation and context for professional growth. The professional literature is replete with theories and empirical studies that underscore the importance of relationship. (See Egan, 2002, pp. 42–44, for a helpful review of reviews in this regard.) For the purposes of this book, we simply review several of the core skills and attributes that support the goal of achieving a simple yet comprehensive framework for doing supervision. Included in this list is the notion of the supportive presence, engagement skills related to psychological and physical attending, listening, empathy, challenging skills, and self-management skills.

A Supportive Presence

Murphy and Dillon (1998) describe a kind of supportive presence that clinicians (and we would offer supervisors) provide that helps facilitate the development of a safe and trusting relationship. They refer to "warmth and caring," "acceptance or unconditional positive regard," and "genuineness or congruence." In addition, they discuss the importance of "availability," "clinical repose," "validation," "affirming strengths," "provision of concrete supports," and "advocacy" (pp. 77–88).

These qualities as well as other personal attributes such as honesty, integrity, thoughtfulness, and sensitivity define a supportive presence and reflect characteristics of good supervisors and clinicians. To strengthen and refine them goes beyond classroom training alone or merely reading about them in a book. Like other behaviors that have to do with character, nurturing a supportive presence requires attention and commitment over time and across situations. Effective supervisors evidence these behaviors, teach their supervisees about them, and continuously model them in the spirit of the dual process. Consider this case illustration, which takes place in the rehabilitation unit of a community hospital:

There is a continuous surge of activity in this very busy rehabilitation clinic where patients are receiving acute care. Many of them are dealing with the losses associated with traumatic injury. The psychiatric nurse practitioner in the clinic, Denise, is extremely dedicated and hardworking. She regularly puts in many hours of overtime, frequently giving patients and their families her home phone number and permission to call at any time. Although she truly wants to be an available and willing support for her patients, there is a kind of frenetic energy she evidences that turns off patients and many staff. Few would describe her as a supportive presence.

Her supervisor, Donna, recognizes her talent and unmistakable dedication to her work. Donna's validation and abiding faith in Denise's strength and spirit is regularly coupled with a call for better self-care and firmer boundaries. She often tries to slow her down, but to no avail—until Denise becomes seriously ill.

Following several months of a successful convalescence, Denise returns to work, rested and changed. While nursing herself back to health, she took time to reflect on the meaning and quality of her interactions with patients and families. She returns with a kind of supportive presence that is more mindful of her pace and the effect it has on her patients and other staff. She monitors her stress levels and takes steps to create clear limits in terms of her time availability for patients and their families, which, ironically, allows her to be more emotionally available for them. The message Donna had been sending in supervision got through.

Did Denise's illness serve as a wake-up call? Did a well-needed break in a burnout pace provide Denise the room to integrate Donna's suggestions and facilitate a shift? Or does this change in some way model Donna's good boundaries and calm and steadying demeanor? Whatever the combination of ingredients, Denise soon becomes a kind of port in a storm for patients and staff alike.

Psychological and Physical Attending

As discussed at length by Egan (2002) and Murphy and Dillon (1998), psychological and physical attending skills are important components that support the initial connection with clients or supervisees. Psychological attending has to do with being present in the moment, a kind of emotional and intellectual availability that is a situational version of the more pervasive supportive presence discussed earlier.

Egan (2002, pp. 67–70) uses the mnemonic S-O-L-E-R to represent physical attending—several types of physical behaviors shown to correlate well with initial engagement. They are "square" (facing the client directly), "open" (maintaining an open physical orientation), "leaning" (leaning slightly toward the client), "eye contact" (effecting appropriate eye contact), and "relaxed" (it is always better for the supervisor to be at least as relaxed as or more relaxed than the supervisee!).

Although these attending skills are generally useful, Zhang (cited in Ivey & Ivey, 1999, p. 36) cautions us to be aware and respectful of cultural differences that call for variations in these general guidelines. He provides graphic examples of how differences in eye contact, touch, physical proximity, and minimal encouragers must be observed when working with Chinese clients. Mary Ivey cautions us in the same citation to adapt other practical and theoretical aspects of our work to people of different backgrounds.

Listening

Many of the relationship skills described in this section facilitate good, clear communication. This is well stated in the old saw, "If you think good communication is all talk, you haven't been listening!" Egan (2002), Murphy and Dillon (1998), Cournoyer (1991), Ivey and Ivey (1999) all discuss various features of good listening. Their reviews vary in depth and range, although each provides some attention to the importance of listening for affective as well as cognitive content. The skilled supervisor should be able to do this as well as teach this skill to the supervisee. Consider this case example.

Spence is a relatively inexperienced marriage counselor. In his weekly supervision meeting with Kathy, his supervisor, he describes an interaction between a husband and wife who work with him as a couple. Spence seems quite irritated as he reports that the wife is highly critical of her husband's work performance. He quotes the husband as saying in response, "I feel she is harsh and unfair. She never has anything positive to say. Tell her to stop."

Kathy asks Spence what he "thinks" is going on in the interaction and how he "feels" about what is said. Spence follows the husband's lead and says he "feels" the wife is indeed being unfair and angrily offers, "He's so right, she should stop criticizing him so harshly." Kathy asks him to listen to her question again more closely and hear the distinction between the words "think" and "feel". She explains to Spence that he may, in fact, think that the wife is acting unfairly, a cognitive process; however, he never really comments on his feeling. Kathy observes that Spence's nonverbal behavior suggests that he does, in fact, feel upset with her. His statement that "she should stop" further suggests his angry feelings.

Kathy processes with Spence his strong feelings and opinions about the wife. She asks him to "think" about the possibility that the strength of his "feelings" may be connected to similar feelings he may experience or have experienced in powerful relationships of his own. Her question has to do with the possibility of countertransference and she reviews this concept with Spence as well as the importance of routinely checking with himself about this possibility as a regular feature of his practice. She suggests that understanding the implications of his thoughts and feelings are a necessary prelude to the behavior choices he must make in deciding about intervention.

(Kathy mentions Rule 1 in this regard, a communication rule I made up for couple clients that distinguishes thoughts or opinions, which are challengeable, from feelings, which are not. Processing both feelings and thoughts should lead to behavior choices that positively and proactively respond to the issues at hand.)

In the spirit of the dual process, Kathy teaches and models for Spence the kind of listening skills useful in this clinical situation as she helps him distinguish between his thoughts, feelings, and behavior. In this case, Spence is encouraged to help the couple do likewise—that is, to process their opinions as distinct from their feelings as a prelude to the decisions they might choose as they deal with their problems.

Empathy

Feeling understood is one of the basic building blocks for fostering trust and safety in both the therapeutic and supervisory relationships. Communicating an understanding of the clients' experience in the clinical relationship (i.e., their thoughts, feelings, and behavior) from *their* perspective helps create an environment for change and growth in much the same way that it does in the supervisory relationship. "Walking a mile in the moccasins" of the supervisee not only communicates empathy but also models empathic behavior in the spirit of the dual process.

Consider this case illustration, in which Manda, the clinical supervisor provides and models empathy for her supervisee, Kip.

In the days shortly following the horrific terrorist bombings of September 11, 2001, Kip reported to his supervisor how inordinately tired he felt. Although he wasn't connected with anyone directly involved in the tragedy, he had trouble concentrating and he found himself weeping in between some therapy sessions. He also became increasingly hesitant to raise questions in the next few supervision meetings, behavior that was highly unusual for this clinician. His supervisor, Manda, recognized that Kip was manifesting many of the signs of secondary trauma. From the choices available to her, Manda first showed great empathy for Kip's feeling and experience, validating his reactions as not only understandable but even somewhat predictable given his extremely sympathetic nature and the tragic circumstances.

Feeling Manda's deep sense of genuine concern and understanding, Kip felt free to discuss why he had been hesitant to talk about his cases. As it turned out, he was feeling a kind survivor guilt in which any worries or questions he had regarding his work paled in comparison to the enormity of 9/11. Manda's empathy not only provided a context that allowed Kip to talk about his experience, but it also paved the way for him to feel permission to discuss his own concerns. Parenthetically, he went on to model this behavior with his clients. A number of them had had similar reactions and several showed a similar hesitation to work on their own issues in therapy.

The nature of empathy in the helping context has been discussed and debated for decades. Readers wishing to study this "trait," "state," "process," "value," "intervention," and/or "communication skill" further are invited to review Barrett-Lennard (1981), Duan and Hill (1996), Egan (2002), and Rogers (1975). Readers are also directed to Kaiser's (1997, Chapter 4) chapter on shared meaning that gets to the essence of empathy in the supervisory relationship.

Challenging Skills

If empathy is the cornerstone of support in relationship development, challenging supervisees may be considered central to the foundation for growth in the development of that relationship. Haynes et al. (2003) cite Corey, Corey, and Callanan who write, "A supervisor's task is to strive for an optimal level of challenge and support. The hope is that the supervisor will promote autonomy without overwhelming the supervisee" (p. 103). Challenging supervisees encompasses skills that bridge islands of experience, feeling, and behavior (after Ivey, 1971; Ivey & Authier, 1978) in a way that goes beyond simple empathy to an understanding and discussion of the *implications* of these thoughts and experiences, feelings, and behavior. Clinicians (in our case, supervisors) construct feedback to clients (supervisees) that may well be outside their awareness, thus stimulating some new understanding in service to change or growth.

Challenges, sometimes referred to as confrontations, can bring blind spots to light (Egan, 2002) as well as discrepancies, inconsistencies, or contradictions in verbal and/or nonverbal behavior (Carkhuff & Anthony, 1979; Egan, 2002; Evans, Hearn, Uhlemann, & Ivey, 1989; Murphy & Dillon, 1998). In the context of supervision, challenging may also entail pointing out ineffective clinical or professional behavior. It is a skill that is usually difficult for clinicians as well as for supervisors, who are regularly called on to utilize challenges in their respective relationships. Often presupposed to be a negative interaction, challenges can be done in a thoughtful and caring way (so as not to overwhelm the supervisee). Some use the terms *caring confrontation* or *carefrontation* (M. Amodeo, personal communication, January 1993).

Including the word *caring* in the term caring confrontation highlights how important it is for supervisors to communicate a basic sense of caring, even when providing feedback that can be discomfiting. (The use of the term *challenge* has also gained increasing appeal in the helping professions instead of the more traditional expression confrontation because, according to Egan, 2002, it has less of an edge. I use both more or less interchangeably in practice and in the text.)

Caring confrontations are never put-downs, nor do they convey an "I caught you" attitude; they relate information from the supervisor's perspective, and supervisors own or take responsibility for their point of view with the use of "I" statements. Supervisors simply point out blind spots and inconsistent or ineffective behavior from their perspective ("I notice that . . . ") and ask if the supervisee has a similar awareness ("I wonder if you see what I see?"). The supervisor invites the supervisee to process observations based on the information at hand while maintaining an open mind to the supervisee's perspective.

Challenges or caring confrontations may be considered one of several intervention skills related to direct feedback that is considered in greater depth in Chapter 6, the chapter that focuses on intervention. Consider this clinical example that illustrates the use of a caring confrontation.

≈≈≈≈≈≈

Jose complains at the start of his supervision session with Marilyn that the chief social worker at the youth detention center is "getting on his case" needlessly. Jose failed to show up for the second of two weekly counseling sessions set up for a newly incarcerated 15-year-old boy. After briefly mentioning this fact, Jose doesn't make any further reference to missing the appointment and begins to strongly argue that he "probably shouldn't have even begun to see this child in the first place because it wasn't clear what catchment area he would be going to when released." (Social workers in that system typically begin working with children before they leave the detention center, but they only work with youth who live in the worker's particular catchment area.)

Marilyn notices that Jose focuses only on the initial contact/catchment question and pays no attention to the issue of his unannounced failure to show. She asks him if he is aware of this, a possible blind spot. The question is delivered with little emotion and in a genuinely inquisitive manner. Jose realizes that he was avoiding talking about that issue, acknowledges it, and quickly (and genuinely) states that he should have called to cancel.

Jose's concern about investing in a relationship that might soon end—disappointing both him and the client—is well founded, but it is not the issue with respect to the cancellation. Further processing reveals that Jose had been angry at the chief social worker because the chief himself had missed several meetings with Jose the previous month without prior notice! Because he hadn't cleared the air with him, Jose is still steamed, and he comes to realize that his unannounced cancellation is a way that he is "acting out" his anger.

At this point in the discussion, Marilyn focuses on some new choice points available to Jose in this situation. His choice is to talk with the chief. This would involve some version of taking responsibility for his own missed appointment first. He then would find out why the chief had missed their appointments (in that order, as Marilyn suggests) and express interest in some kind of reconciliation. They could then both focus on the underlying systems issue regarding initial meetings and proper catchment areas.

<hr>

Marilyn's caring confrontation begins with a simple observation and a request that Jose reflect on what his perspective is regarding the unannounced cancellation. Because Marilyn is nonjudgmental and specific in her observation of his behavior, Jose is freed up to consider more closely what he is saying and doing, and he takes responsibility for his feelings and actions. When considering ways to address the problem with the chief social worker, Jose follows Marilyn's suggestion to take responsibility for his own behavior first. It raises the likelihood that the chief will be responsive in the ensuing discussion, particularly if Jose follows with a "caring confrontation" of his own. Marilyn suggests that he simply share his observations about the chief's missed meetings and genuinely request the chief's perspective.

Notice how Marilyn's challenge to Jose becomes a model he can use to challenge the chief. (Challenging skills are not exclusively reserved for the domain of supervision and counseling. They are skills that are useful in *any* relationship that calls for communication about differences in perception, feelings, values, or behavior.) Marilyn's skilled intervention, coupled with the existence of an ongoing and trusting relationship between supervisor and supervisee, facilitates Jose's forthcoming communication with her and helps make the ensuing brainstorm about what to do a relatively straightforward and productive process.

Jose, on the other hand, does not have as positive a history with the chief, and the challenge is much trickier. Paramount to the success of his challenge with the chief will be Jose's ability to experience and project a set of emotions that are receptive to some kind of reconciliation. To do that, Jose must be skillful in managing his feelings, thoughts, and behavior in this complex relationship. In the next section, we review several methods Jose can use that may help.

Self-Management Skills

"That thoughtless chief social worker blew off our appointment; I feel so angry, I can't stand it." "Some feeling is blocking me from talking about my cases. This is not like me. I feel my own resistance." "There is something about that supervisee that I don't like, I just can't put my finger on it."

As we work with others as clinicians, supervisors, or supervisees, colleagues, we are guaranteed to experience a variety of feelings across a number of difficult circumstances like the ones expressed above; these will require some kind of thoughtful response to the people involved. As supervisors, the responses we choose in relation to the feelings we have for our supervisees (and they for their clients) can have a profound effect on the level of trust and safety in our supervisory and clinical relationships. As such, it is important to use, teach, and model successful methods that supervisees can learn and use to manage their feelings, thoughts, and behavior effectively. By facilitating this kind of learning, the hope is that supervisees will eventually integrate these methods for use on their own as they learn to self-supervise. The following ideas can help build such self-management skills.

We begin by considering ways to manage our feelings as supervisors (and help supervisees manage theirs) in two typical circumstances. The first concerns acting on feelings that are outside of our awareness (sometimes called "acting out"); the second relates to managing emotions that are so strong (e.g., anxiety and anger) that we have a hard time acting on them thoughtfully. The obvious first step in managing feelings outside of awareness is to clearly identify what they are and bring them into awareness. The traditional expression that is used is to get in touch with our feelings. This involves some version of assessing and accurately labeling our internal affective experience. (The expression is used frequently in the helping professions but less frequently defined for newer supervisees.)

Supervisors help supervisees get in touch with their feelings by processing the events and circumstances related to their feelings using the core skills we have been discussing. In the last three case illustrations, we see examples of how supervisors use the requisite core skills to help their supervisees identify their feelings in order to deal more effectively with clients and colleagues. In the case of Kathy and Spence, for example, Kathy *listens* for affect with Spence and teaches him to do likewise with his clients. (Remember Rule 1 from that case, which distinguishes between thoughts, feelings, and behavior. Getting in touch with our feelings is often a prerequisite to making effective choices about what behavior we want to choose in a particular situation.) Kathy also defines and discusses the notion of countertransference with him, a frequent dynamic in clinical work. Managing one's countertransference demands evaluation of one's emotional experience to tease out reactions specific to the client compared to feelings transferred from other significant relationships. (We discuss this further in Chapter 6.)

Manda's *empathy* for Kip gives him permission and room to identify and acknowledge his sense of survivor guilt, feelings that had been outside his awareness and for which he previously had had no label. Validating and naming these feelings frees him up to discuss his clients with her, getting past a kind of resistance that blocks his work (and provides a model for him to do likewise with his clients). Her skill here is oriented to helping him be in touch with his feelings, in service to his professional growth, even though he may benefit personally.

In the last case discussed, Marilyn *challenges* Jose to think about why he avoided discussing his unannounced cancellation with the chief social worker and helps him get in touch with his unrecognized feelings of anger. By doing so, Jose has the opportunity to make a thoughtful choice as he considers the behavior he will use to challenge the chief—a response, in this case, modeled after the behavior Marilyn uses with him.

In each of these circumstances, the supervisor uses core skills to teach and model ways their supervisees can get in touch with their emotions. Once supervisees are aware of their feelings, they can generally make more thoughtful choices about what to do with them. Consistent with the role of facilitating professional growth, supervisors engage in these processes and label them for their supervisees so that they eventually internalize these approaches and utilize these self-management skills on their own.

There are times when supervisors and their supervisees *are* in touch with their feelings, but there emotions are so powerful that they find it hard to make thoughtful decisions about a course of action. Supervisors can use, teach, and model several methods to manage such strong emotions. One method is to suggest taking an "adult time out"—that is, to remove oneself from a hot situation and allow for a cooling off period (similar to the ones used in labor negotiations). This usually provides enough time to think out (instead of act out) an appropriate course of action.

Another way to manage strong feelings is to restructure the ways we *think* about them and to engage in productive self-talk (Ellis 1962; Goldfried & Davison 1976; Meichenbaum & Cameron, 1974). For example, we can challenge ourselves (using the appropriate self-statements) and our supervisees (teaching them how to make appropriate self-statements) to consider the other person's perspective in conflictual situations. (I call this the "your perspective, your perspective, perspective"—no typo here—for want of a better description). The "other person" may and probably does have information we don't have that could affect how we feel and consequently what we do. Even with the same information, there may well be a valid point of view we have not yet considered (and probably should). Restructuring our cognitions can temper our emotions and create conditions that allow for more mindful behavior choices. Thus, how we choose to behave, how we manage our feelings, can be mediated by how we *think*.

These skills provide a fairly straightforward framework for self-management we can use, teach, and model for our supervisees. Implementing each step along the way can be very difficult. (There is no claim here for an easy application!) Rest assured that it can be quite a challenge to properly identify our feelings, think mindfully about our options, and choose effective ways to act on the alternatives chosen. But we are clinicians. This is what we do.

CULTURAL COMPETENCE

In the context of supervision, cultural competence has to do with the supervisors' ability to effectively relate to the diversity of their supervisees and to facilitate a process whereby supervisees do likewise with their clients. In recent years, there has been a proliferation of literature related to cultural competence and multiculturalism. But as Haynes, Corey, and Moulton (2003) observe, "there is little information available regarding multicultural practice in supervision" (p. 134).

Despite the paucity of literature directly related to multicultural supervision and cultural competency, it is useful to outline some basic ideas that are being discussed and extrapolate several principles from the broader literature that apply to our discussion of supervisor skills and attributes. In this section, we first review some definitions and a brief outline of several basic models of cultural competency with multicultural clients and supervisees. This foundation provides a context for further discussion in this and other chapters of the book. We then return to the focus of this chapter as we highlight ways that supervisors can competently develop safe and trusting relationships in a multicultural context. We carry through our discussion of cultural competency in Chapter 4 as it relates to assessment, Chapter 5 as it relates to problem identification, and Chapter 6 as it relates to intervention.

Definitions and Culturally Competent Practice Models

Lum (1999) has conceptualized a culturally competent practice model that can be applied to supervision. He offers this simple working definition: "The term *cultural competency* describes the set of knowledge and skills that a social worker must develop in order to be effective with multicultural clients" (p. 3). Fong (2001) reiterates Lum's definition of cultural competency and defines *multicultural* as a term whose meaning has been broadening in the field such that it "addresses varying facets of culture, which include race, gender, age, sexual orientation, religion, and so on" (p. 4).

A definition of multicultural that utilizes this broader perspective of culture also is applied to supervision by Haynes et al. (2003, p. 134), who cite Pederson:

> By defining culture broadly, to include within-group demographic
> variables (e.g. age, sex, and place of residence), status variables (e.g., social,
> educational, and economic), and affiliations (formal and informal), as well

as ethnographic variables such as nationality, ethnicity, language, and religion, the construct *multicultural* becomes generic to all counseling relationships. (p. 36)

In explaining his model, Lum (1999) discusses cultural competency as a performance outcome related to the attainment of cultural awareness, knowledge acquisition, skill development, and continuous inductive learning; these are the ways practitioners can come to be more effective with multicultural clients. Beginning with cultural self-awareness, Lum suggests that practitioners become more successful as they gain insight from understanding their own ethnic and cultural roots as well as having contact with "ethnic others." Acquiring knowledge and skills in relation to multicultural clients provides boundary guidelines for direct practice and service delivery, and competent practitioners continue their personal learning process by uncovering facts about multicultural clients inductively.

Haynes et al. (2003, pp. 132–150) outline and discuss a number of components they believe to be part of competent multicultural supervision that are consistent with Lum's suggestions for competent practice with clients:

- Explore racial dynamics in the supervisory relationship
- Include multicultural competencies in the supervisory agreement
- Assist supervisees in developing cultural self-awareness
- Accept your limits as a multicultural supervisor
- Model cultural sensitivity
- Accept responsibility to provide knowledge regarding cultural diversity
- Inform supervisees about multicultural considerations in assessment
- Practice and promote culturally appropriate interventions
- Provide and promote social advocacy

Haynes et al. have also adapted a conceptualization of multicultural counseling competencies for use by supervisors that is based on the work of Arredondo and her colleagues (1996) and Sue and his colleagues (1998). They specify attitudes and beliefs, knowledge, and skills necessary to effect three distinct performance outcomes for supervisors (reprinted in its entirety in Appendix A):

1. Being Aware of Your Own Cultural Values and Biases
2. Understanding the Worldview of Clients and Supervisees
3. Developing Culturally Appropriate Intervention Strategies and Techniques

Readers wishing to review these models in greater detail are directed to Lum's book, *Culturally Competent Practice* (1999), and the chapter, "Becoming a Multiculturally Competent Supervisor" in Haynes et al.'s book, *Clinical Supervision in the Helping Professions,* (2003, chap. 6). We now turn from these broader conceptualizations of cultural competency to a more focused discussion of attributes and skills that help build trust and safety in the developing relationship.

Culturally Competent Relationship-Building Skills
and Attributes

Kaiser (1997), whom we referred to earlier in our discussion of empathy, emphasizes the importance of "shared meaning" between supervisor and supervisee as "the grease that allows the smooth running of the supervisory relationship" (p. 88). She says that "challenges of cross-cultural supervision are most evident in the area of shared meaning" and the "greater the differences between supervisor and supervisee, the greater is the possibility for blocks in the achievement of shared meaning" (p. 89).

Consider this case example, which provides an excellent illustration of how difficult it can be to attain shared meaning cross-culturally:

In a recent supervision session conducted at a neighborhood counseling center, Robert was responding to a question from an African American supervisee who wanted to know more about psychosis. He had just begun to work with a young African American client, who, in addition to reports of frequent hallucinations, talked continuously about his wish to "make beats." The supervisee noted that his client was quite immobilized and wasn't doing anything "to make that happen." As a middle-aged "white guy," Robert's immediate thoughts (and words) went to a question related to food instead of music: "How could he even 'make beets' in the first place?"

Talk about shared meaning! How can we as supervisors competently increase the likelihood of attaining shared meaning in a complex relationship that by its very nature involves *differences* (sometimes great differences!) of cultural experiences, norms, beliefs, needs, and behaviors? At the same time, we must model and teach our supervisees to do likewise with their clients in the spirit of the dual process! These are central issues regarding cultural competency and multiculturalism that stand before us, as we talk about the skills and attributes necessary to develop safe and trusting relationships.

Obviously, there are no simple answers. Cultural competency does, however, begin with *commitment* (Egan, 2002, p. 49, uses the words *radical commitment*). We must be committed to raising awareness and consciousness and truly thinking about and valuing diversity in our clients, our supervisees and ourselves as suggested in the models reviewed above: commitment to acquiring information in an ongoing way; commitment to learning the skills over time that can differentially apply the knowledge we have acquired as various situations dictate. After all is said and done, more is said than done! "Talking the talk" is one thing; "walking the walk" beyond the commitment is another.

To aid in this endeavor, features of cultural competence associated with relationship development are highlighted below, punctuating the more general considerations we outline in the last section. Discussion begins with a summary of Lum's (2000) "contact stage" as set forth in his process stage approach to working with people of color (this is supplemented by a helpful series of direct questions that Haynes et al., 2003, use to discuss multicultural considerations early in the supervisory process). We adapt features of Lum's extensive framework in this and later chapters by keying in on several of the practice process stages he writes about in his book. (Lum also writes extensively about worker-system practice issues, client-system practice issues, and worker-client tasks in each stage; the interested reader is encouraged to review these for an in-depth study.)

A review of the "ethnographic stance and interview" as summarized by Anderson (1997) follows next and completes this section. This method and several related communications skills attendant to this approach help the clinician (and supervisor) learn about the worldview of clients and supervisees from their perspective in a way that facilitates increased trust and safety.

When reading about these approaches in the next few pages, notice how some relationship-building methods emphasize skills that relate to *common features shared across cultures.* This is sometimes referred to in the literature either as a universal approach (Haynes et al., 2003, pp. 134–135) or an etic approach, which, according to Lum (2000, p. 129), "documents principles valid in all cultures and establishes theoretical bases for comparing human behavior" (citing Brislin).

This universal or etic approach may be compared to what Haynes et al. refer to as a broad approach that *focuses on multicultural identity* as defined in terms of a broad understanding of culture: appropriate ethnographic, demographic, status, and affiliation factors. Lum refers to this as an "emic" approach that "documents behavioral principles within a culture and focuses on what people themselves value as important and familiar to them" (p. 129).

Lum's Process Stage Approach: Contact

Lum (2000) lays the groundwork for his contact stage by advocating relationship skills that relate universally to all clients, and in addition, focus on a broadly defined cultural identity of a particular client.

> The worker should discover the etic and emic characteristics of the client and cultural background during contact and relationship building. In a real sense, the worker communicates the message that the client is a human being with basic needs and aspirations (etic perspective) but is also a part of a particular cultural and ethnic group (emic perspective). Moving between these two points of reference is a creative experience for both worker and client. (pp. 130–131)

Lum says that the main tasks of the contact stage involve *nurturing* and *understanding.* From the etic or universal perspective, he advocates the use of the core skills we have been discussing to successfully effect these tasks: empathy, warmth, and genuineness; listening and understanding; spontaneity and openness; and respect and concern for the client as a human being (pp. 131–132).

From the emic perspective, Lum suggests that the practitioner learn about the client's personal and family background, degree of acculturation, and in essence, their multicultural identity. Focused questions can help the practitioner gain an understanding of the client's worldview and nurture him or her. Genuine interest, for example, in the client's ethnicity can build trust and safety and "may be an important signal to a client that his or her ethnicity is valuable information" (p. 132). Lum offers the following as examples of the kinds of questions clinicians can ask (p. 132):

- How do you identify yourself as a member of an ethnic group?
- What important ethnic customs and beliefs do you and your family observe and practice?
- Are you a participant in ethnic organizations? What are your favorite ethnic foods?
- Whom do you consider to be a local spokesperson or leader in your ethnic community?
- Are there any ethnic groups or individuals you would approach for assistance?

Asking questions like these may be particularly important for clients who are entering a system unfamiliar to them, staffed by people who are unfamiliar to them and whose multicultural identity may also be unfamiliar. In this last respect, Lum suggests that the practitioner "practice professional self-disclosure, which personalizes the relationship and fosters rapport and trust" (p. 329).

As mentioned, Lum's framework is aimed at working with clients. As supervisors, it is important for us to understand it, teach it, and model it for our supervisees so that they may effectively put these ideas into practice with their clients. It is also important to put these ideas into practice with *them*. The best way to model these skills and understandings (in the spirit of the dual process) is to utilize these principles in relation to our supervisees. Haynes et al. (2003) suggest that supervisors begin a dialogue about multicultural considerations with supervisees early in the supervisory relationship, many of which can help build safety and trust as well as foster awareness about the importance of these principles. Listed below are a range of suggested questions that can initiate that dialogue (p.139):

- How do you describe your ethnic identity?
- What does it mean to you to identify with this group?
- If you were to think about the multiple layers of culture, what would you identify as the various cultural groups to which you belong?
- Can you identify, at this time, ways in which our cultural differences or similarities may affect our supervisory relationship? How would you rate yourself in terms of knowledge and comfort when discussing cultural issues?
- If you find cultural discussions uncomfortable, can you identify what it is you find awkward or threatening? Where might you have learned that fear?

Being tuned into and picking up on opportunities that present themselves in the course of supervision can complement initiating discussion about multicultural considerations directly. Consider the following case example in which a group supervisor seizes the moment to facilitate trust and safety and build relationships in a racially and ethnically mixed group of bachelors'-level counselors. The members work in a multiservice agency counseling neighborhood middle and high school students. They have been meeting each week with a supervisor who had been working in another part of the agency for a long time but has been working with this newly formed group for only a few months.

Following a general check in with members of the group, Elwyn has the floor and reports struggling in his work with a 16-year-old student who had been regularly truant from high school and threatening to quit altogether. The boy is extremely bright and does well when he attends, but he feels the weight of financial pressures at home and manages to slip in extra hours at work during the days he's out of school. Elwyn's difficulty, he explains to the group, has less to do with the student's problems than with his own; he thinks he is making good progress toward the goals he and the student have set out together. His struggle, he says, has more to do with managing some of his own feelings, which are reminiscent of feelings he had experienced when he was in high school.

The supervisor believes Elwyn is taking a big risk with the group. Up to this point in time, the group members have focused primarily on the content of their cases, and the supervisor is well aware that he is forging into new territory. Moving slowly and respectfully, he asks Elwyn if he would like to talk about what those feeling are. Elwyn, who is a dark-skinned young man born in Portugal and of Cape Verdian descent, explains that his work brings back painful memories of not fitting in when he was a student.

His high school was racially mixed with a fairly equal proportion of White kids, Black kids, and Portuguese kids. "The White kids thought of me as Black, the Black kids thought of me as Portuguese, and the Portuguese kids thought of me as Cape Verdian—and there were very few Cape Verdians in the school. I was having enough trouble just figuring out what it meant to be a teenager (his family immigrated to the United States when he was 8), much less one that didn't fit in anywhere. Just walking around the high school these days brings back those feelings to me."

The supervisor expresses gratitude to Elwyn for breaking the ice and talking about his cultural background and how it relates to his feelings about doing the work. He acknowledges that they haven't discussed their multicultural differences as a group up to this point (and maybe should have). He asks Elwyn if he thinks it would be helpful to hear from other group members. He agrees. The supervisor asks the group if anything Elwyn says resonates with their own experience, and if so, to share what they do to manage their feelings, if they think it will help. The group has members of African American descent, several with a Hispanic background from Puerto Rico and the Dominican Republic, a Cambodian, and several White people with Eastern European backgrounds.

In short order, other members of the group eagerly begin to share similar experiences and feelings about not fitting in; some talk about times they felt discriminated against. They also speak further to the supervisor's question and talk about a variety of ways that they have learned to take care of themselves in spite of their feelings and experiences. Elwyn's verbal and nonverbal behavior signals that he feels their support and understanding; when asked, he responds, "This helps."

Much of the rest of this session is spent learning about features of everyone's cultural heritage. The supervisor is deliberate about inviting each member to share (although it is clear that there is no pressure to do so), and he takes a position as learner as members teach him and the others in the group about their experiences and worldview. The supervisor also relates a relevant feature about his own cultural background (disclosing that both his parents are native Spanish speaking, yet at the same time, he is also of Jewish heritage). He points out the richness of the many layers of culture group members bring with them into this group. In checking out Elwyn's take on the session as well as the impressions if other group members, the members generally acknowledge that they are getting what they need from the group at this time.

Consistent with Lum's suggestions, the supervisor in this case example is focused on understanding and nurturance. He provides room for Elwyn to discuss his feelings and share important information about who he is in this fairly early stage of the group's development. Elwyn takes a risk and is treated well, so the level of trust and safety in the group increases. The supervisor moves to strengthen relationships further by creating a framework that invites others to empathize with Elwyn and provide feedback if they have experiences that resonate with his—which is likely, given the makeup of the group. By framing his invitation in this way, he provides an expanded forum in which they can share more about themselves with the group.

The supervisor is genuinely interested in the ethnicity and background of group members, and he takes an "ethnographic stance" by taking the position of learner with respect to the multicultural information group members choose to share as teachers (we discuss this method further in the next section). The supervisor discloses something about his own cultural background, as Lum suggests, and uses the opportunity to teach the group about the concept of multicultural layers in that context and the richness it brings to the group experience. These choices both model and teach cultural competence.

This group is in the initial stage of group development, and the supervisor takes the opportunity to build trust and safety as beginning relationships strengthen. He makes the choice point to focus on multiculturalism for this group meeting and facilitate self-sharing; time is not spent on case content for this session. Following a check in, the group does its work, and the supervisor checks out with them to see whether they are getting what they need, a kind of communication about the communication in the group (called metacommunication). These and other points about group process are discussed more fully in the next chapter.

The Ethnographic Stance and Interview

Anderson (1997) talks about the ethnographic stance as a kind of attitude the clinician adopts to better understand the multicultural differences of the client and, in the spirit of the dual process here, the supervisee. He says, "The ethnographic stance places us in the role of the learner and the client or group member in the role of the authority" (p. 63). He credits Lofland (1971) for defining the "ethnographic interview" that Anderson says "is a major tool in the ethnographic stance." He summarizes it as "a process of discovery by which the interviewer proposes to ask focusing questions designed to channel his or her learning and the interviewee serves as the expert to guide the learner through his or her culture" (p. 64).

The process of learning from the client or supervisee by virtue of the ethnographic stance and interview can increase the sense of shared meaning. It respectfully demonstrates a desire to *really* understand, and this in turn can help strengthen trust and safety in the relationship. The supervisor in the last case example uses this method to learn about the multicultural background of members of his supervision group. He does this in a way that prizes the richness of their experience, and he provides space for group members to share at a pace that feels right for them, without pressuring them to supply information just to meet the learning needs of the supervisor or group members—an important point to note.

Anderson (1997, pp. 64–65) reviews techniques used in the interview citing Lofland (1971), Spradley (1979), Austin, Kopp, and Smith (1986), and Kochman (1981). He summarizes their work by saying, "The specific techniques for this are to ask persons to talk in their own terms, use their own language, and permit the asking of questions about the meaning of these terms. . . . The learning comes from sensitive listening with both the eyes and ears" (p. 64).

Anderson refers to Gudykunst's (1991) chapter titled "Effective Communications with Strangers" (pp. 34–41), which suggests several associated communication principles pertinent to the ethnographic interview. Gudykunst stresses effective listening (essentially active listening) and the use of feedback to share observations and evaluations to learn whether information is correctly understood. He further suggests the use of explicit metacommunication (after Watslawick et al., 1967), which involves communicating about the nature of the communication itself to determine whether there is a successful transfer of information.

Anderson (1997) writes an extremely cogent and insightful summary of this approach, which ties in well to our discussion of cultural competence with multicultural clients and supervisees in the engagement phase:

> In this ethnographic stance to communication we avoid assumptions, seek relevant data, ask questions before drawing conclusions, and share our

conclusions with clients or group members to "check out" our understanding. We learn about the nature of the community in which the person lives and about the person's way of perceiving, thinking, and acting. We learn what differences appear to make the most difference to the client from his or her perspective. For the moment, in using an ethnographic approach, the learning is not necessarily focused on the person's problems or immediate goal. The underlying motive for the dialogue is to achieve a better understanding of the member's ethnographic perspective. (p. 64)

ETHICAL USE OF SELF

Ethics relates to conduct that governs behavior while engaging in professional practice. Each of the major helping professions puts forth its own version of a code of ethics, which is a set of ethical principles and/or standards that expresses the values of their members in the form of guidelines for appropriate professional behavior. Supervisors are responsible for ensuring that supervisees understand and adhere to the professional code of ethics under which they practice.

Although all codes are different, most have several guidelines in common. We briefly review informed consent and due process to begin this section, having already referred to them when discussing the supervisory contract in the last chapter. We then examine several ethics constructs based on values that directly influence the development of a safe and trusting atmosphere for supervision. We briefly outline confidentiality first, followed by a discussion of the ethical use of power and ethical caring. Attention to boundary decisions that involve the potential for multiple or dual roles and relationships (*not* to be confused with the dual process) completes the chapter.

We return to a discussion of ethics in Chapter 6 when we examine several principles of ethical practice that also have legal implications. Not only do codes of ethics provide criteria for the ethical choices that supervisors and supervisees make in practice, but they also frequently serve as benchmarks for legal evaluations of professional behavior (Levy, 1993). Therefore, we examine the notions of the standard of care and abandonment, and return to a discussion of confidentiality and the limits of confidentiality with respect to legal obligations that relate to the duties to warn, protect, and report. We consider other key features of the legal system that relate to supervisory practice and ethics as well and discuss a method of ethical decision making that supervisors can use (and teach their supervisees to use) to help them deal with ethical dilemmas.

Informed Consent and Due Process

We referred to informed consent and due process in the context of the supervisory contract in the last chapter. According to Falvey (2002), "Informed consent provides parties with the information they need to make decisions about their participation in specific activities" (p. 70). Both supervisees and supervisors make decisions to work with one another in a variety of ways and both consent to the contract that clarifies what those ways are and what is expected of them (e.g., roles, learning objectives, responsibilities). Supervisees agree in the contract to provide clients with the opportunity to be informed as well—about the nature of their treatment and the fact that supervision is involved—before they consent to the work. (Readers interested in a more detailed study of informed consent are referred to Falvey's chapter 6, pp. 70–75.)

The notion of due process is also mentioned in the context of the contract, as the supervisee is informed about due process rights mainly in relation to periodic feedback and evaluation (e.g., in formative assessments and summative evaluations—discussed further in Chapters 5 and 7.) Due process is derived from the 14th Amendment and refers to the rights and procedures used to challenge decisions or judgments that are considered unfair, usually in relation to academic or job performance in the supervisory context. According to Falvey (pp. 112–116), a variety of responses are appropriate in different work settings, and she provides an excellent review for those interested in greater detail. We turn now to the issue of confidentiality as it relates to trust and safety in the developing supervisory relationship.

Confidentiality

Confidentiality and the limits of confidentiality are key ethical considerations supervisors must observe in their relationships with supervisees (and ensure in the relationships supervisees have with their clients). Unforeseen breaks in confidentiality can and usually do have traumatic implications for the level of trust and safety in these relationships. Falvey (2002, p. 92) says, "Perhaps no other aspect of therapy evokes as much anguish for professionals as our struggles over when, if, and how a client's right to confidentiality may be limited in a given situation." She quotes Adrienne Rich in this regard (originally quoted in Pope & Vasquez, 1998): "When we discover that someone we trusted can be trusted no longer, it forces us to reexamine the whole instinct and concept of trust. For a while, we are thrust back into some bleak, jutting ledge . . . in a world before kinship, or naming, or tenderness exist" (p. 92).

Circumstances that could lead to a breach in confidentiality should be anticipated, even if the consequences of a break do not appear to be as compelling as suggested in Rich's quote. Consider Erin's thoughtfulness as she anticipates the possibility of just such a breach related to her supervisory work with a counselor and that counselor's supervisor.

———

Erin is a psychologist who facilitates several private supervision groups on an ongoing basis. She also frequently consults at various social service agencies. She was recently asked to provide individual supervision to a supervisor at one of these agencies who happened to be the supervisor of a drug and alcohol counselor in one of Erin's private groups. Both counselors were very experienced and got along quite well, wanted Erin's supervision, yet were also aware that there could be a conflict of interest with respect to privacy and confidentiality—a potential dilemma. In a meeting with the three parties, they decided that any concerns regarding the two workers would be off limits for discussion. Erin would be available, however, to mediate mutually agreed upon issues with them conjointly, in the unlikely event of their occurrence.

We return to a discussion of the limits of confidentiality in Chapter 7, which concentrates on more complicated situations involving the legal mandates to warn, protect, and report.

Use of Power and Ethical Caring

In her comprehensive discussion of "power and involvement in supervision relationships," Holloway (1995, pp. 42–49) reviews how power has historically been considered as power over or domination in educational settings. She cites Follett (1924/1951), who introduced the concept of "power with" and suggests that this "basis for power is more consistent with psychotherapy and supervision, where the intent is not to control, but rather, to empower individuals to exercise self-control and determination" (p. 44). Thus, if supervisors wish to achieve an atmosphere of safety and trust in which supervisees and clients feel empowered and free to reveal inner experiences with a minimum of vulnerability, they then must not exercise *power over* but *power with*.

Learning to "power with" and demonstrate what Noddings (1984) refers to as *ethical caring* is sometimes easier said than done even for the most experienced practitioner or supervisor. Kaiser (1997) relates that Noddings distinguishes between natural and ethical caring. Kaiser writes, "*Natural caring* refers to situations in which we act on behalf of someone else because we want to. *Ethical caring* is called for when we need to act in a caring way but don't feel a natural inclination to do so" (p.75). Consider the case of Harry and Sally.

Sally is a well-trained, highly ethical adoption worker, who was helping Peg and Dan set up an adoption plan for their two-month-old daughter. Peg and Dan clearly felt overwhelmed raising their three other children. Even though they were receiving a great deal of help from Dan's parents, they decided that adoption would be best for this child and for them. While setting up the plan, the couple made it clear that they wanted someone outside of the immediate family to raise this child. This was not an unusual request, and Sally planned to set up the paperwork and facilitate a search for adoptive parents.

That was her plan until she met Dan's parents. She "fell in love" with the way they loved this child. They expressed an unflinching desire to adopt, despite the crystal clear wishes of their children, the birth parents. Sally couldn't help but feel that they were the right people to parent this child. "The way they looked at this little girl convinced me that they were the ones."

Harry, Sally's supervisor, instantly saw the conflict of interests in this case when it came up during their regular supervision session. He pointed out to Sally that Peg and Dan were her primary clients. Unfortunately, he then directed her to promptly effect a search for outside adoptive parents. The two workers became polarized. Sally believed Dan's parents should have been considered major candidates as adopters. Harry pressed for an immediate outside search. Sally felt vulnerable and controlled because Harry came on so strong.

She felt he was ordering her around and using his "power over" her even though they had previously had a fairly trusting and collegial relationship as seasoned professionals. In fact, they had formed a kind special bond in their relationship over the years as others kidded them about their names in light of Billy Crystal and Meg Ryan's movie. Nevertheless, Sally and Harry dug in their heels.

Harry, at first, felt nervous and out of control when he saw how strongly Sally had overidentified with Dan's parents; he believed she had not fully considered the implications of this possible adoption for the birth parents and feared she would press the birth parents to reconsider their decision. As Sally balked at his directives, Harry dug in further.

Fortunately for both clinicians and most importantly for their clients, cooler heads prevailed. In fact, those cooler heads were Harry and Sally's! Harry realized that the intensity of his feelings and behavior was overpowering Sally and sabotaging her sense of professional independence. His anxiety initially blocked him from communicating with Sally, or "powering with" her in a way that showed trust in her ability to consider all implications until the proper course of action emerged. Despite his initial feelings, Harry did back off and apologized for his pushy behavior at the start of their next supervision meeting.

By that next meeting, Sally, too, had softened. She had learned more about the family as she took additional time to discover why Peg and Dan felt so strongly about their wishes for an outside adoption. Given this additional information, she was more than ready to "power with" Harry, especially in light of his conciliatory manner. Working together, they eventually fashioned an open adoption plan in a way that satisfied all in the family and actually strengthened the supervisory relationship.

Although he didn't fully feel like it at first, Harry backed off his over powering stance and took responsibility for pressuring Sally. He did this out of an obligation to treat her with integrity, if not initially by natural inclination. Thus, he evidenced "ethical caring" as discussed above. Supervisors often feel anxiety in situations like this because they are legally responsible for the actions of their supervisees. Because they feel out of control, they are tempted to use the authority of their position to regain control by using the inherent power differential of their position to "power over" their supervisees. The supervisor may get his or her way with respect to a particular decision, but if the supervisor uses this authority across situations and over time, the very basis of trust and safety will be eroded—if it was ever there to begin with.

Collaborative methods, which focus on sharing power interdependently, create and support trust and safety in the engagement process. Beyond that, it also philosophically underlies many of the strength-based approaches suggested in the rest of our framework for supervision. These approaches are consistent with some of the concepts associated with feminist models, as reviewed by Haynes, Corey, and Moulton (2003, pp. 122–123):

> The supervision process is clearly explained to supervisees from the beginning, which increases the chances that the supervisee will become an active partner in this learning process (Corey, 2001c). The feminist model of supervision entails striving toward an equalization of the power base between the supervisor and the supervisee. Although the supervisory relationship cannot be entirely equal, the supervisor shares power in the relationship by creating a collaborative partnership with supervisees. The supervisor-supervisee relationship is based on empowerment. Supervisors do this by modeling how to identify and use power appropriately. (p. 122)

"Powering with" and demonstrating "ethical caring" are clearly ethical methods that promote the development of the supervisory relationship. We turn our attention now to ethical principles related to boundary issues and "dual" or "multiple" relationships, which are intended to preserve their integrity.

Dual Relationships and Boundary Decisions

No discussion about the ethical use of self in developing safe and trusting relationships would be complete without discussing boundary decisions that relate to dual or multiple relationships or roles. As Bernard and Goodyear (1998) point out, "Ethical standards of all mental health disciplines strongly advise that dual relationships, or engaging in relationships in addition to the professional relationship, between therapists and clients be avoided" (p. 187). A similar case can be made for the supervisory relationship; like the therapeutic relationship, there is an inherent power differential in the supervisory relationship that can overtly or subtly exploit the supervisee if power is misused or appropriate boundaries crossed (Haynes et al., 2003).

Unlike therapeutic relationships, however, supervisors often find themselves in a variety of settings and in dual or multiple roles with supervisees, which may create boundary confusion between the two. For example, both may work in the same agency over time and find that they serve on the same committee together, have the same superior, and engage in work-sponsored social activities or work together on an event in the community. In the last chapter, we discuss several role functions (teaching, advising, mentoring, consulting) that require supervisors to be particularly clear in their boundaries as they switch gears from one function to the next.

Kaiser (1997, pp. 61–86) devotes an entire chapter to power and dual roles in supervisory relationships. She suggests that success in dual relationships also depends on the supervisors' expertise in using their inherent power appropriately. Citing Peterson (1992, 1993a, 1993b; Storm, Peterson, & Tomm, 1997), she suggests that the existence of a dual relationship is not so much the issue as a *covert* "dual agenda in the relationship, whether or not a literal dual relationship exists" (p. 64). Kaiser provides a good example:

> The overt or official agenda is the attention to the supervisee's needs, and the covert agenda is the attention to the supervisor's needs. For example, a supervisor may give a supervisee information about a colleague with the expressed goal of helping the supervisee deal with that person more effectively. The covert agenda may be that the supervisor is hoping to form an allegiance with the supervisee in a conflict with a colleague. . . . This situation creates confusion for the supervisee, who feels powerful and special because of being asked to meet the supervisor's needs, and who at the same time feels diminished because those needs are in competition with his or her own. (pp. 64–65)

The potential for abuse exists unless the needs of the supervisee are considered first and foremost regardless of the myriad of settings and roles in which supervisor and supervisee find themselves. It is inevitable that there will be role ambiguity and boundary confusion between supervisors and supervisees under certain circumstances. Living with that blurring of roles is a simple fact of life. When handled openly and ethically, however, the very foundation of trust and safety in the relationship can be protected and even strengthened. For readers interested in a more comprehensive discussion, please see Bernard and Goodyear (1998, pp. 187–192) Falvey (2002, pp. 79–83), and Haynes et al. (2003, pp. 164–181).

3

※

The Individual
and Group Formats
for Supervision

This chapter on individual and group formats for supervision completes our discussion of the engagement phase in supervision. As supervisors discuss roles during a period of orientation and negotiate learning objectives, responsibilities and criteria for success in the initial supervisory contract, they also set up the structure for individual and/or group supervision sessions (depending on the work setting). Each format provides a somewhat different forum to help structure the supervisory process as supervisors and supervisees move into the work phase. As mentioned earlier, these features are discussed with the supervisee throughout the relationship.

THE FORMAT FOR INDIVIDUAL
SUPERVISION

There is no one way to organize the process and structure of the individual supervision session in the work phase; however, several principles may help frame a way to think about this format. Although there can be great variation in the content, the *process and structure* of the individual session as suggested here can be fairly predictable and organized with consistency as supervision moves through to the work phase. Individual sessions start with a check in at the beginning of each meeting that leads to session goals, the work itself, and finally, the check out.

The supervisor usually begins the check in informally by asking the supervisee "how things have been going" since they last met. This kind of open-ended question gives supervisees room to talk about what might be uppermost in their minds and lets supervisors do a quick temperature check on where they are. Much can be learned about what is most salient for the supervisee at this moment by what is said (or not said) in what has been called the "golden five minutes." For example, some supervisees get right to business (especially if they are paying for a professional consultation!). Some use this time to avoid getting to business, which could signal the possibility of some resistance, and some supervisees, stylistically, need to make a transition to the work through social small talk. By tuning in to what is important to their supervisees, supervisors respectfully send the message that their work is an important collaboration that *starts* with the supervisees. (This process also helps to build trust and safety in the relationship—continuing throughout the supervision.)

Having checked on the supervisee's current status, the supervisor begins to establish session goals with her or him. Session goals are those goals agreed on for a particular supervision meeting. They are negotiated near the start of each meeting and essentially set the agenda for that meeting. Both the supervisor and supervisee initiate agenda items that reflect old business left over from previous meetings and new business that might or might not have been the focus of the golden five minutes.

Session goals are generally anchored to the respective roles of supervisor and supervisee as well as the learning objectives, responsibilities, and criteria for success agreed to in the supervisory contract. They also tie into assessments, evaluations, goals for growth, interventions, and/or renegotiations of the supervisory contract as related to current clinical work with clients or in relation to administrative issues (we talk more about these when we talk about the work phase in Part II).

A typical session goal initiated by a supervisee might include a request to consider several clinical practice questions and practice a new skill related to the answers. Or there might be a request for the supervisor to assess a videotaped segment of a therapy session to give the supervisee feedback and to discuss strategy for the next session. (Imbedded in these session goals is an understanding that the supervisor's role is to facilitate learning through this feedback so that supervisees gain knowledge, improve skills, and strengthen their professional attitudes and values.)

Another example of a session goal, initiated by the supervisor, might be to establish a goal for growth with the supervisee based on problems observed during several earlier assessments. The supervisor might also suggest a session goal to review several strengths that had been observed in order to reinforce "what works" and help establish clarity about strengths for the purpose of evaluation. In addition to clinical issues, session goals may also reflect content and questions about ethics, cultural competence, agency policy and service delivery, licensing requirements, systems concerns, stress on the job, and other matters.

After agreeing on the session goals, the supervisory pair does the work to accomplish these goals (teaching, learning, empowering, assessing, setting new goals for growth, intervening, evaluating, etc.). Whether the work is related to assessment, a fine point about an intervention the supervisor seizes upon during a teachable moment, refining a basic goal, or adding a more specific one, it is always connected to session goals and anchored in the supervisory contract.

Periodic discussion about the process and structure of the session itself (sometimes called *metacommunication*) is helpful to ensure that the supervisor and supervisee are on the same page and successfully tracking progress according to agreements in the contract. This discussion is often included as part of the check out, which is initiated toward the end of each session. The check out is also a time to summarize the work of the session by reviewing the "take-aways" (major learning points the supervisee takes away from the session); it can also provide a valuable opportunity to integrate what was learned during the session. Sufficient time should be allowed during the check out to plan for the next meeting as well as review the current one.

Before discussing the group supervision format, we return to the case of Sam and Dave who themselves have progressed to the work phase in supervision. In reading this case example, notice how Dave uses the basic process and structure of the individual session as suggested above to organize the meeting. Also notice how the work is connected to the supervisory contract. The main session goal is to review a videotape Sam brings into the session, provide feedback to him about his clinical skills while doing family therapy, and consider several questions about his work that he prepared prior to the supervision meeting.

Sam is finishing his third month at the Family Service Agency and has just begun to see his first family therapy case there. He had requested the opportunity to learn about and do solution-focused family therapy and he specified a basic goal related to this request in his initial supervisory contract. Dave, his supervisor, was happy to oblige.

Sam received permission from the family to bring a small segment of videotape to the weekly supervision session. He has seen the family three times and they are pleased that they will get the "extra help" from the supervisor. During the check out at the end of the last session, Dave suggested that Sam review the tape before their next session. He suggested also that he note what he believed to be his problems and strengths, what he might do differently if he could redo the therapy session (sometimes called a "second take"), and prepare questions he would like considered in the meeting with Dave.

Dave checks in with Sam about how things are going and what session goals he is interested in for today. Following up on the last session, Sam says that for the main agenda item he would like to review the tape from his family session and get some feedback. To begin, they agree to watch a 10-minute segment of tape Sam chose in preparation for today's session and see it straight through without comment.

It is clear that Sam has had experience working with families as his engagement skills are excellent and he appears to be relatively relaxed. When asked about this observation, Sam reveals that he was "shaking in his boots"; both are glad that Sam doesn't appear as nervous as he felt ("better to look good than to feel good, and you look marvelous!").

Dave invites Sam to comment on what he has observed and ask his questions. (Dave had been cueing him the last few sessions on ways to come prepared for supervision and Sam is increasingly using supervision time more effectively.) Dave also sees progress in Sam's ability to be introspective and evaluate himself, and Dave comments on this as well as on the sophistication of several of his questions. Sam's main concern, as he puts it, is his "difficulty convincing this family of the strengths that they, in fact, do have."

The pair rewinds the tape and watches Sam as he recounts the family's progress and points out their many strengths. He's right. There doesn't seem to be any traction, and Sam is met with a series of "yes, buts . . ." Dave debates whether to draw Sam out by suggesting *he* come up with other choice points for intervention or simply review some techniques he knows to be useful in this situation (such as "scaling questions"— discussed later in the text), and then spend time practicing them. He decides on the latter because Sam tends to learn best when concrete experiences and active experimentation are emphasized. (See our discussion about Kolb's "learning styles" in the next chapter.)

Dave also makes this decision because he is concerned that time might run out in the session. (He admits to a pang of guilt at making a supervision decision based on expediency, but he fears that otherwise there will be no time left to hear other observations and questions.) After some behavior rehearsal, Sam and Dave go through other sections of the tape and discuss some of Sam's "second takes"—what he would do if he had a chance to redo portions of his session. Dave particularly likes this method of working with videotape. "This work is plenty hard," he quips, "actors get the chance to do videotape replays even with the advantage of starting out with a script! So why not us?"

Toward the end of their time, they review the learning takeaways for the session and Dave checks out with Sam to learn whether he got what he needed (a kind of "mini" metacommunication, or discussion about their discussion). They briefly plan their next meeting. Sam will report on several cases they haven't discussed lately, and they will begin a general review of Sam's problems and strengths in relation to his learning objectives (a formative assessment) in anticipation of his end of semester summative evaluation. Dave enjoys the good humor they have together and at the end of the session, after congratulating him for his hard work, he refers to Sam's first question of the day and jokingly reminds him that it's rarely a good idea to attempt "convincing" any client about anything.

Serious as the work is, Dave inserts moments of appropriate humor to keep Sam's stress level down in this session. Doing and reviewing a video for the first time can be a daunting task for any clinician regardless of developmental level, and Dave knows enough about Sam at this point to guess that he may be shaking a bit in his boots about this session (to use his words) as well as in his work with the family. His suggestion that Sam consider ways he would redo portions of the tape if he could is not only designed to stimulate thinking about alternative interventions, but it is also designed to provide a supportive atmosphere for him; this is reflected in Dave's statement about how hard it is to work "without a script." (Further suggestions will be made about the use of videotape in the next chapter's section on direct methods of assessment.)

Sam and Dave's interaction in the case example reflects a supervisory relationship in which both parties are engaged and involved in the work phase. An advantage of the individual supervision format is that it allows attention to be focused on the needs of the supervisee and gives the relationship room to develop in a forum more private than group supervision. In the next section, we consider group supervision and compare several advantages and disadvantages of each format as part of that discussion.

THE FORMAT FOR GROUP SUPERVISION

At the most basic level, supervision conducted in a group is similar to individual supervision except that it is conducted in a group format. The supervisor utilizes many of the individual supervision skills, knowledge bases, and professional values we talk about throughout the book. Group supervision complements individual supervision and provides another forum in which to implement the roles, learning objectives, and responsibilities agreed to in the supervisory contract. Using this format in the clinical setting, however, requires knowledge and skill in setting up the appropriate group structure and managing the group process.

There are several different kinds of groups in clinical settings that serve different purposes. Two of these, staff meetings and training groups, encompass some of the administrative responsibilities of many clinical supervisors, and we discuss some of these implications for managers. We briefly describe these among other kinds of groups before highlighting group clinical supervision more extensively in its own section. In that section, we describe the mind-set (i.e., the cognitive or mental set) of the supervisor who prepares practically and psychologically to run a group, outline the stages of group development, and discuss the structure and process of the group clinical supervision session as it is conducted in practice. Because clinicians and trainees who are interested in doing group clinical supervision often ask for the words used to orient participants in an initial meeting, we illustrate the process and structure in a case example. Finally, we summarize the advantages and disadvantages of group compared to individual supervision.

KINDS OF GROUPS IN
THE CLINICAL SETTING

The Staff Meeting

One sort of group in the clinical setting is organized around basic administrative type issues and is often presumed to focus on the agency's needs. Clinical supervisors who serve as managers are frequently in charge, particularly in smaller agencies, even though their primary function may be clinical supervision. This group is often simply called a staff meeting, and the structure of the group is typically organized around an agenda that communicates information about policies and procedures, service delivery, productivity, coverage, record keeping and other issues related to risk management and managed care, announcements about changes, and so on.

Although these agenda items are typical to most staff meetings, the process by which supervisors facilitate communication in them offers a number of possibilities. Because the staff meeting is a "group," it is subject to many of the same dynamics seen in other, more obvious group situations. Therefore, it is wise to facilitate this group process with attention to the needs of group members *as well as* those of the agency. This can be difficult, particularly when supervisors are asked to implement agency directives that may seem to be at odds with the wishes of the staff. Supervisors often feel caught in the middle and are frequently heard to complain that they are either squeezed by those above them in the hierarchy, or squeezed by those below. And they often are! We discuss the dilemmas of the middle manager further in Chapter 7 and describe a win/win negotiating strategy that helps manage the fit between the needs of the agency and the needs of the staff member/supervisee.

The Training Group and Utilization Review

The training group is often organized in relation to the agency's staff development goals. These kinds of groups may include didactic seminars centering on specific clinical matters or issue-oriented sessions and tutorials of interest to the staff (e.g., on safety, managing managed care, etc.). They may be conducted by supervisors, staff members, or outside consultants. Training groups conducted in medical settings are often referred to as *grand rounds*.

An interesting kind of training group has begun to emerge in many social agencies, borrowing organizational structures predominant in other kinds of businesses. This group is formally set up by the agency's management team with a name like "utilization review" (UR) or "quality assurance" (QA) and usually serves a training function that can include aspects of staff development and/or quality control, depending on the agency. Members of the group review cases together, issues of service delivery, and similar matters in a regular meeting that is sanctioned by the hierarchy of the agency yet is not directly a part of it. These groups offer a unique opportunity to affect the culture of the organization "outside the lines" of the agency's hierarchy as creative ideas and information frequently come out of these sessions.

The spirit of this approach derives from the Total Quality Management (TQM) movement in management that shares the classic managerial functions of planning, organizing, leading, and controlling with *nonsupervisory* employees (Stahl, 1995). Agencies that adopt a TQM approach emphasize employee involvement (similar to the use of quality circles so prevalent in Japan) and deemphasize hierarchy. The reader is referred to Stahl (1995) for a more in-depth review.

Peer Supervision

Peer supervision (or peer consultation as it is sometimes called) is a group composed of students, trainees, and/or professionals who, unlike UR type groups, *informally* agree among themselves to come together for the purpose of strengthening their practice and providing mutual support. These groups are conducted in or out of agency settings and meet without the services of a designated supervisor. The substance of the groups is usually quite similar to that of group clinical supervision without the evaluative feature.

Group Clinical Consultation

A group clinical consultation is also quite similar to group clinical supervision as the actual structure and process of the two groups can virtually be the same. Part of the consultants' role is similar, too, as the consultants fulfill educative and supportive functions. The main difference is that the consultant is not typically a regular, full-time employee or a member of the agency's hierarchy. There are several other differences as well.

Consultants to agencies assume a different level of responsibility from that of the regular supervisor who monitors the day-to-day quality of services provided to clients. (This is also true of consultants doing individual consultation.) Although consultants are particularly mindful of the needs and welfare of clients, the picture they see is a snapshot that can change more quickly than their availability. They are generally hired for periodic group consultations and are simply not present often enough to track changes in client progress as the regular supervisor does.

The group clinical consultant is also generally not responsible for fulfilling any or many of the administrative responsibilities expected of the regular supervisor, such as conducting formative assessments and summative evaluations, negotiating the fit between the supervisee's needs and the needs of the agency, and so on. The limited availability of these consultants precludes such functions, as does the focus of their work. Consultants generally focus on problem solving more difficult case situations, systems issues, or multicultural and ethical questions, and there is an expectation that they are not only accomplished as supervisors but also have the proficiency to impart expert clinical advice.

GROUP CLINICAL SUPERVISION

As mentioned above, group clinical supervision shares many of the features of other groups in the clinical setting and individual supervision. Similar to individual clinical supervision, the major focus is to facilitate professional growth. It is "most simply . . . defined as supervision in a group format" (Kadushin & Harkness, 2002, p. 390).

Even so, this format requires an additional set of understandings and skills. For example, the supervisor has the responsibility of managing group process and all the dynamics attendant on normal group development. The supervisee is receiving supervision in a more public forum and has additional responsibilities and ground rules to follow as a "good" group member. This format also involves a generally higher level of risk and exposure as well as an expectation of good social skills, which are needed to manage group interaction—for supervisor and supervisee alike. The challenges can be great but the results can also be highly rewarding for both.

We highlight group clinical supervision in this section, and review several group dynamics including preparation for the group, the stages of group development, and the process and structure of the group clinical supervision format. It is beyond the scope of this book to provide a thorough study of group dynamics. For an in-depth review, the reader is referred to the works of Anderson (1997), Bernard and Goodyear (1998), Corey and Corey (2002), Kadushin and Harkness (2002), and Yalom (1995).

Preparing for the Group: The Supervisor's Mind-Set

Supervising more than one person at a time can be a daunting task, and supervisors should prepare themselves psychologically and practically to deal with the additional challenges. Group clinical supervision requires the same kinds of knowledge and skills necessary to do individual supervision, but the format demands a kind of on-stage presence needed to work with more than one person at a time. And the work is not with just a collection of individuals. Kadushin and Harkness (2002) warn that supervisors

> have to move from an accustomed focus on the individual as the center of interest to perceiving the group entity as the center of concern. If a supervisor cannot successfully reorient his or her focus, he or she may become engaged in an individual supervisory conference in the group context. The tendency might be to respond to a collection of individuals rather than to the group. (p. 401)

One way to reorient one's focus and get mentally prepared is to reflect on the questions posed below in advance of running the actual group. They are organized in five categories (patterned after Corey and Corey, 2002, pp. 98–110, and Munson 2002, p. 203): type of group and population; reasons for the group; goals and criteria for success; practical, practice and process questions; and evaluation.

- *Type of Group and Population:* Who will this group be for? Staff; students; various combinations and permutations of supervisors, experienced clinicians, and rookies? What is the cultural mix and what are the implications of such a mix? Will it be strictly billed as "group clinical supervision" or will it have some of the administrative aspects of a staff meeting and/or didactic aspects of a training group?

- *Reasons for the Group:* Why is there a need for such a group? How will this group be a contribution? Does your rationale go beyond saving time? What are the advantages and disadvantages compared to individual supervision?

- *Goals and Criteria for Success:* What outcomes are desirable for group members and the agency? Are the goals different from those for individual supervision? What will tell you that you are successful? Are objectives specific enough, measurable, and attainable in the time allowed?

- *Practical, Practice, and Process Questions:* What methods will be used to screen for membership, if any? How large will the group be and will new members be welcome after it has started? How often will it meet, for how long and where? What will be the duration of the group? Will it be open-ended, time limited? What will be the ground rules for the group? Will they be determined solely by the supervisor or include some degree of consultation from group members? What methods, techniques, and approaches will be used to facilitate professional growth and provide a supportive atmosphere? How will group process be similar or dissimilar to individual supervision? How will discussion about the structure and process of the group be initiated? (We focus on this in the next section).

- *Evaluation:* What methods will be used to evaluate the effectiveness of the group? Will they account for the criteria for success established at the beginning of the group? How will the performance of supervisees be used for formative assessments and summative evaluations, if at all?

Asking and answering these questions provide a level of readiness that can help the supervisor prepare for the group. Knowing something about the typical stages of group development can also help supervisors prepare for what "might be coming around the corner." As Corey and Corey (2002, p. 94) suggest, "Understanding the typical patterns during different stages of a group will give you a valuable perspective and help you predict problems and intervene in appropriate and timely ways." We consider this next.

Stages of Group Development

There are stages and processes that are more or less predictable in every group; this includes group clinical supervision. Corey and Corey (2002, p. 94), tell us that "knowledge of the critical turning points in a group can guide you in helping participants mobilize their resources to successfully meet the tasks facing them at each stage." Bernard and Goodyear (1998, p.119) cite Tuckman and Jenson who they say have the most "recognized model of group development."

They refer to the stages in these terms: "forming, norming, storming, performing and adjourning." Anderson (1997) uses the acronym TACIT to describe the sequential steps in task group development and problem solving. Corey and Corey (2002) describe the "initial, transition, working and ending stages" of group development, and Haynes, Corey, and Moultan (2003) apply this outline to group supervision.

We integrate several important features of group development here from among these models. Each model is different, of course; however, threads that run through them demonstrate conceptual similarity. First, some kind of preparation for the group is suggested, this includes decisions about how the group is to be set up, clear rationales, and objectives, as we discuss in the last section. This sets the stage for the actual group process. The first or initial stage of the group itself generally involves some kind of orientation, discussion of objectives and ground rules as well as relationship building and development of trust and safety ("forming"). Haynes et al. (2003) reiterate the supervisory contract in this stage and urge that supervisees become actively engaged in forming the agenda for each subsequent session.

Behavior in the next stage (Corey and Corey's transition stage) can involve resistance, limit testing, or competition between members ("storming"), and there may be performance anxiety and testing to see whether supervisors create an atmosphere safe enough to take risks. Group cohesion is strengthened as conflicts and resistance are resolved ("norming") and the group transitions to the work stage as group members then do the work for which the group was intended ("performing").

Groups members raise questions about case situations, ethical questions, multicultural concerns, systems issues, the experience of doing the work, and the group process in the work stage, and they give and receive feedback to and from each other and the supervisor in an increasingly supportive environment. The group finally moves into an ending or termination stage ("adjourning") where there is usually validation and consolidation for what has been learned. Evaluations are completed and the group members do the work of separation and termination.

Process and Structure of the Group Session

Having prepared himself or herself practically and psychologically to begin doing group clinical supervision, the supervisor is ready to initiate the group. Supervisors begin by outlining a kind of contract or informed consent that is similar to the supervisory contract. They review roles, goals, or learning objectives for a particular group, and the responsibility members take as they agree to certain ground rules and the format for group process.

In the case illustration below, notice how the supervisor familiarizes the group with the kinds of issues appropriate for discussion, certain ground rules related to the group setting, and the process by which the work proceeds. The actual sequence parallels the individual session with a check in, the work itself as related to session goals, and a check out. Special attention is given to the unique dynamics of the group format, however, and the supervisor is explicit about the heavy emphasis placed on building trust and safety.

⌖⌖⌖⌖⌖

Every time Dot starts a new supervision group she feels a bit anxious, but tonight, she is mainly excited. She *knows* these five people because they are all in individual supervision with her, and they are all basically dedicated clinicians. She has prepared well for this group and reflects on the groups she has facilitated in the past as well as the ones she's been in during her years in practice. In true strength-based fashion she mostly reflects on the good times and the ways she managed to work through the challenges during the bad. (She remembers a quote attributed to Samuel Clemens, "Good judgment is born of experience, and experience is born of bad judgment." What will this experience bring?)

The group is composed of newer staff in this large community mental health center, most of whom have had several years post-masters' experience doing individual, child, and family counseling. She reminds herself before beginning that even though all these clinicians have experience, they may not have any experience being group members or know anything about group supervision.

Dot starts off welcoming the members of the group and makes sure they all know each other. She is happy to have the opportunity to "cross-fertilize" individual sessions with group and vice versa; it will give her an opportunity to see her supervisees in a different context and bring group discussions back to individual supervision when useful. Dot soon addresses the group with an agenda of the session goals for this meeting.

She explains that there are four major goals for tonight's two-hour session: the first is to familiarize the group with the kinds of issues appropriate to discuss; the second is to set some ground rules; the third is to provide a picture of how the group looks when it is "in process." Fourth, she looks for the group to begin building trust as they start getting to know each other as a group. In addition, she hopes that there will be time left to review a case or some other issue. She begins with an outline of the kinds of issues appropriate for the group to consider.

One type of issue involves clinical practice questions related to the cases people are working on. Discussion and feedback might focus on questions about relationship development; role induction; the clinical contract; assessment; goal setting and criteria for success; intervention and evaluation as well as the knowledge, skills and professional attitudes and values related to them. (She wonders to herself if she should have written all this down for the group, but she realizes that they have frequently heard this in their individual supervision sessions with her, particularly when discussing learning objectives in their supervisory contracts. The focus on this kind of content in both formats is essentially the same.)

Dot summarizes several other kinds of issues that might take the attention of the group. These include ethical questions, questions related to multicultural practice, and large systems questions that either relate directly to their cases or may stimulate appropriate large system interventions. A newer staff member, unfamiliar with the notion of a large system intervention, asks Dot to give an example of how that might relate to his work with clients as a therapist. Dot is delighted that Barry takes the risk to ask this basic question early in the life of the group.

She briefly explains a systems perspective and gives an example related to a question that came up in Barry's individual supervision that week. He did an intake with the parents of a little girl who had been told that she was having problems with several other children in class. In reviewing the case, Dot had suggested to Barry that he talk directly with the teacher about this child's behavior and observe her in class before interviewing her. Learning about the impact of other people in the child's "system" would enhance his assessment; subsequent suggestions to the teacher following assessment could lead to a more effective intervention on behalf of the child. Dot explains that this is an example of a "large system" intervention that directly relates to a case. She also ties in her knowledge of Barry's work on a voter registration campaign as an example of a large systems intervention that does not have direct impact on his therapy but affects the welfare of many of his clients.

Dot checks out with Barry to make sure she answers his question and thanks him for taking the risk to speak up. She also talks about the possibilities for a supportive atmosphere in the group, one in which people feel free to ask questions and share their mistakes as well as the inner experience of doing this kind of demanding work. She explains that when group members take risks and are treated well, the likelihood that they will take more risks increases. Should they continue to treat each other well, this virtuous circle should result in an increasingly safe and trustworthy environment.

Having taken a brief but relevant detour from the order of her agenda (she was going to talk about a supportive process in the group later), Dot returns to another type of issue supervision groups sometimes discuss: questions about service delivery. She explains that "group soup," as group member Ellen has started to call it, is an appropriate arena in which to talk about the system of service delivery as it affects both clients and staff. (Realizing that discussions about service delivery and other policies set by the agency can turn into unproductive gripe sessions, Dot uses this topic to transition into a discussion about ground rules.)

She notes that discussion about service delivery brings up one of several ground rules she will ask group members to honor. It is from her supervisor, who calls it "Bob's rule": No complaints without proactivity! "I've been there too many times. We start talking about a service delivery problem and whammo, we're spending the rest of the session griping about all that's wrong with the agency, or managed care, or how the agency is not managing managed care. Sharing is fine. Venting is fine. Seeking validation for your experience is fine. Stopping there is *not* fine. We have a number of ways to be proactive about what I'm sure will be your excellent observations. There are staff meetings, committees, even special task groups that lobby for change at the state capital. And we will help you stratergize. So, can we agree on this rule?"

Dot makes it hard not to agree with ground rules. She likes to think that she is flexible (and she is about most things), but her boundaries are quite firm in this department. So, while she is at it, she decides to share a few other ground rules with the group before moving to her last session goal regarding a typical group process. (Her goal about trust building is already in process.) First, Dot makes several strong points about confidentiality and its limits. She then spends time listening to the group wrestle with what those limits should be, occasionally joining them in the ring. Shelly shares her thoughts in relation to some excellent interventions that she made with a family involved with the state's protective services agency and her decision to break confidentiality in service to the protection of a minor and her duty to report.

Following this discussion, Dot revisits the point or rule about taking risks and treating each other well. She understands that group members may feel anxious and vulnerable about sharing their work with others in so public a forum, particularly near the beginning of the group before trust and safety are established. She shares her hopefulness that members will take the chance to raise their concerns about their own work in the group, as well as give feedback to others about their work and the group process itself.

She notes that group members, like clients, will do best when feedback is provided with liberal use of the "core relationship skills" that they are always talking about. In the same vein, she mentions her wish that the group be an error accepting environment and once again, implores them to share their mistakes. "This is the place, this is the time! It's hard for all of us to share our mistakes . . . good judgment is born of experience, experience is born of bad judgment." She shares every platitude she can think of to normalize what many group members may be feeling and set a tone oriented to taking risks and creating safety, ending with "If you take risks, and are treated well, you will take more." (She thinks to herself, "Ah, the joys of overkill." She feels a bit funny about punctuating these points so powerfully in so compact a period of time, but good judgment is born of experience and . . .)

Dot turns to her last session goal for the night, which is to paint a picture of how the group process typically proceeds. (About an hour has passed and Dot still hopes to get to at least one case or another issue before their time is up.) She explains to the group that the first order of business is to check in. "We go around the room and usually take three or four minutes to check in—in outline form—about any cases or issues that you're puzzling over. This is parallel to the establishment of the session goals we set up at the start of individual supervision meetings.

"You may have a practice question about a case or one that isn't exactly tied to a case but calls for some conceptual information. Or, you may have a question or concern about this group's process, or about an ethical issue, multicultural practice, large systems or service delivery, or something else, as we discussed earlier. Your check in may also include an update from some previous issues the group has dealt with or news about something you would like us to know about (a conference you've attended, receiving your license, getting some new responsibility in the agency). Although we are not well set up at the moment, we will soon have the capability to tape and do live supervision, and there will be times that you can request feedback from us as we watch you work live or on tape.

"If you would like to have some focused time from the group, put the issue on the table and we'll come back to it after everyone checks in. The reason we wait until everyone checks in is because sometimes there's a pretty heavy agenda and we have to sort out those cases or issues that seem to be most pressing from the point of view of the group member. Also, there are times when cases or issues dovetail with each other and we can combine our discussion. When group members haven't had a chance to present lately, they get priority.

"After we decide on the priorities for the session and it's your turn, do a short presentation related to your issue and if you know what you want from the group, ask for it in the form of a question. That doesn't mean you have to know what your question is. For example, people sometimes just want to talk about a case situation that they are confused about and look to the group for help in figuring out their question! We aim to please. Take a chance.

"After you give your presentation and provide guidance to the group about what you want, I will usually open up the discussion for group consideration. People usually ask some questions for clarification and frame their feedback in ways that respond to your question. I will take responsibility to tie together the group's feedback and add my take. You'll notice that there are times that I'll just jump right in with little or no time for the group. When I do that, it's usually because we're pressed for time, and I want everyone who wants a turn to have one."

Realizing that she is pressed for time at that very moment, Dot concludes her summary of the group process by mentioning the check out as an opportunity for group members to comment on the process of the group, summarize takeaways, and plan for the next meeting—a format similar to the one used in the individual session. After answering a few clarifying questions, Dot notes that there is no time left for any focused work or an adequate check out. She apologizes, and Elissa, who can have a wry sense of humor at times, turns to Adam at that moment and says (in a voice loud enough for everyone to hear), "You'd think with all those years of experience she could have at least slipped in a case or two, and allow us enough time to properly check out!" Dot thinks and says aloud, "I'm gonna like this group."

⌾⌾⌾⌾⌾⌾

Dot pretty much covers all the bases she wants to touch and more or less stays to the session goals she had set out. At the same time, she gives herself permission to deviate from her agenda in order to provide examples or punctuate points she believes to be important. For example, she spends a fair amount of time illustrating Barry's question about large systems interventions because she believes that clinicians who mainly work as counselors should understand the connection their work has to the larger system.

By bringing in a case Barry was already working on to illustrate her explanation, Dot uses the advantage she has of complementing individual sessions with group supervision as a kind of cross-fertilization across learning environments (next we discuss other advantages as well as disadvantages of group compared to individual supervision). She thanks Barry for taking his "risk" to ask this question (whether he experienced it as a risk or not!), so as to emphasize from the very start how important she believes it is for group members to feel and to be free to ask questions in this "error accepting environment."

When Dot takes Elissa's comment about her poor time management gracefully and with good humor at the end of the session, she reinforces the idea that she, too, can and will make mistakes, and that that is okay. By virtue of her nondefensive response, Dot also sends the message to the group that she is secure in her position as group leader. Her reaction could allay fears new group members sometimes have about the competence of the person in charge.

ADVANTAGES AND DISADVANTAGES
OF GROUP COMPARED
TO INDIVIDUAL SUPERVISION

There are both advantages and disadvantages in providing supervision in a group. We briefly outline them here and direct the reader to two excellent reviews from which this overview is taken. See Bernard and Goodyear (1998, pp. 112–115) and Kadushin and Harkness (2002, pp. 391–403) for two thorough analyses.

Advantages
1. Groups allow for a greater economy of time, money, effort, and expertise.
2. Supervisees have more of an opportunity to be exposed to a wider range of client situations and to learn vicariously from the experiences of their peers.

3. Feedback from fellow supervisees can generate a rich variety and diversity of perspective that may also be easily understood and internalized because peers communicate it.

4. Groups can act as a source of emotional support and encouragement for members and can provide an opportunity for group cohesion, team building, and/or a sense of "belonging" to the unit or agency.

5. Groups can provide a forum that allows for power sharing and lateral teaching of peers, which can facilitate independent thinking and behavior.

6. Because supervisees are working in a peer group, they have a way to evaluate their own progress in the context of their peers' experience. Supervisors also have the chance to gain a more comprehensive picture of the supervisee than is possible in individual supervision alone.

7. The group setting allows supervisees who work with groups to use the supervisor as a model and mirror successful interventions (in the spirit of the dual process!).

8. Group supervision can facilitate creative assessment and intervention activities such as action-oriented behavior rehearsal and open consultations.

Disadvantages

1. The group format may not allow supervisees the time and individualized attention required to meet their personal learning needs.

2. Great variability among group members in terms of their interests, relevance to their practice, and skill levels can limit the usefulness of this format.

3. Certain group dynamics can impede learning, such as competition or scapegoating among members. Also, the group may develop norms that preclude creative independent thought or diminish the opinions of a minority of members or new members to the group.

4. Supervisors are challenged to choose explanations and teaching techniques that are inclusive of the learning styles, cultural identities, and developmental levels of a group of individuals—a daunting task when working with just one!

5. Confidentiality is less secure in groups both in terms of clients and the supervisees themselves.

This section has reviewed essential features of both individual and group formats for supervision. Given the preponderance of advantages and disadvantages inherent in both individual and group approaches, it is helpful to consider their use in a complementary way. Kadushin and Harkness (2002, pp. 402) summarized this point extremely well:

> Because both individual and group supervision provide special advantages and disadvantages, because both are more or less appropriate in response to different conditions and different needs, it is desirable to employ them as planned complementary procedures. Frequently the agenda for group conferences derives from recurrent problems discussed in individual

conferences; often, the group discussions are subsequently referred to in individual conferences on individual supervisee case situations. The flow is circular. . . . Because the same supervisor is generally responsible for both individual and group conferences, the two different procedures can have unity and continuity. The supervisor has the responsibility of determining how each approach can best be used to further the learning needs of individual supervisees.

PART II

🌿

The Work Phase

Building on Engagement

Orientation has been completed, roles are becoming clear, and learning objectives, action plans, criteria for success, and clinical and adminsitrative responsibilities in the inital supervisory contract have been negotiated. Supervisees are scheduling and seeing clients, and the style that supervisors use to organize the structure and process of individual and group sessions is becoming familiar to newer and more experienced supervisees alike. Throughout engagement supervisors work to build trust and safety in the developing relationship as they utilize a variety of core relationship skills and practice in ways that are culturally competent and ethical.

They continue to use these skills and develop the relationship in the work phase, of course, as the focus shifts more directly to the supervisees' work with clients. As supervisors assess their work with clients, they to get to know their supervisees and their clinical (and administrative) work more fully. In the first part of Chapter 4, we discuss how supervisors learn more about their supervisee's mulitcultural attributes, experience, development level, and learning styles as a context for assessment and feedback going forward in the work phase. In the second section, we focus on a variety of direct and indirect methods that can be used to discover information about the supervisees' problems and strengths.

As problems and strengths are assessed in relation to clinical (and/or administrative reponsibilities), feedback is regularly presented and summarized in the form of an evaluation called the formative assessment. The supervisory pair determines specific goals for growth based on findings from the assessment, and they establish an action plan and criteria for success in order to build on strengths and remediate problems. Supervisor and supervisee revise the supervisory contract and determine whether goals for growth add to learning objectives, and modify or replace some of them as they relate to clinical and/or administrative responsibilities and expectations for service. These processes are fully explained in Chapter 5.

Chapter 6 focuses on clinical intervention possibilities; this completes the work phase with the supervisor in his or her role as facilitator of professional growth. These possibilities center on educational, empowerment, core skills, and culturally competent interventions. Chapter 7 completes the work phase as it focuses on intervention possibilities relating to the supervisor's administrative role as a manager. These interventions include the supervisor's responsibilities for managing risk as well as the responsibility to help fit the needs of the agency with the needs of the supervisee/staff member.

Please remember that relationship development, contract negotiation, assessment, goal setting, and intervention are often occurring *simultaneously* in dynamic fashion. We separate our discussion of each here because writing is a linear process and requires this kind of sequential analysis and because the discussion does reflect a more or less accurate guide to how these process phases develop.

We now begin discussion of the work phase, starting with assessment.

4

※

Assessment

As supervisees schedule and see clients, supervisors begin to focus more attention on the assessment of their clinical responsibilities (and as managers, their administrative responsibilities). Spending time with supervisees from engagement into the work phase, supervisors assess their range of knowledge, skills, professional values, and attitudes as well as the personal attributes they bring into the supervisory relationship. Supervisees bring unique skills and attributes to the work, which provides a context that guides the supervisor's decisions in each stage of the work phase. In this regard, we continue to deepen our understanding of supervisees' multicultural attributes; consider the implications of their experience and level of development; and come to understand the influence their learning styles can have on the supervisor's choices for intervention. We discuss these variables in the first part of this chapter.

An important part of the assessment focuses on collecting information about the supervisees' effectiveness in their work with clients. This is a discovery process that assesses for problems and strengths. Supervisors acknowledge, punctuate, and build on the resources and strengths supervisees bring with them as a cornerstone of the supervisory process. At the same time, supervisees at *every* level of expertise have room to grow (we assume that clinical work involves a *lifelong* learning process). Thus, the assessment also involves discovery, acknowledgment, and attention to problems and limitations in the supervisees' work.

Assessment provides the basis for providing feedback, and as supervisors, we are not shy in sharing "our take" as we and our supervisees move together toward professional growth. Lum (1999, p. 9) cites Hepworth, Rooney, and

Larsen who note: "Competency must thus be viewed within a temporal context, for a practitioner may achieve competence at one time only to suffer steady erosion of that competence by failing to keep abreast of ever-expanding knowledge and skills." Building on our understanding of what supervisees bring to the table, we use a variety of direct and indirect methods of assessment to learn more fully about their clinical work, so that our observation is more fully informed. We discuss these methods in the second part of the chapter.

MULTICULTURAL ATTRIBUTES, EXPERIENCE AND DEVELOPMENT LEVEL, AND LEARNING STYLE

Multicultural Attributes

During the contact stage, discussed in Chapter 2, supervisors focus on understanding their supervisee's multicultural identity as they develop and nurture the supervisory relationship. Supervisors are authentically interested in and appreciate the supervisee's culture, and they utilize several methods to learn more about it. They use methods such as ethnographic interviewing, the use of direct questions, and sensitivity to opportunities for contact in the course of supervisory sessions. These approaches also serve as a model for supervisees who are learning to build relationships with their clients in culturally competent ways.

Relationship building continues into the work phase and supervisors use similar methods to conduct ongoing assessments of their multicultural supervisees as they help them learn more about and make competent assessments of their multicultural clients—in the spirit of the dual process. In this section, we carry through our outline of Lum's (2000) practice process stages adapting those parts that apply to supervision. In this section, we focus on his definition of assessment and the meaning of the term *cultural assets*; we also delineate several specific categories that can be used to gain information important in making skilled assessments. In addition, we illustrate several methods supervisors use to get this information.

Lum's Process Stage Approach: Assessment Lum (2000) defines assessment in multicultural practice as the "estimation or determination of the significance, importance or value of resources" (p. 218). He takes a strengths perspective and defines the resources clients (and in our case, supervisees) possess as their "cultural assets," which provide a powerful context that contributes to their ability to cope. He refers to the importance of family in this regard as well as "personal or religious belief systems, survival skills, natural healing practices, [and] community networks" (p. 218).

Assessing for and valuing the cultural assets supervisees bring into the supervisory relationship is important for several reasons. It continues to help develop trust and safety in the supervisory relationship by validating the richness of their experience. It also models an important feature of assessment they can use with their clients, and provides the supervisor with greater understanding of who they are so the supervisor can help them see how their personal resources can be an asset as they serve their clients. Consider the following example of a discouraged counselor who works in a neighborhood drop-in center as he discusses his frustration on the job.

Orlando begins his weekly meeting with his supervisor, Winton, by checking in about a youth he works with who had been arrested for selling marijuana. He is feeling down about the daily battle he wages against the local drug dealers, who compete with him for the futures of these young men. He is extremely insightful about what he calls, "this highly sophisticated family type business that recruits kids by offering them fast cash, the protection and camaraderie of the group, and a short life span—they just don't advertise the short life span part." Orlando grew up in a similar neighborhood and freely talks about having won the battle for himself, with the help of a strong extended family and the Christian Brothers who run a similar drop-in center in his parish. During the three months this young Latino man has been working at this center, Winton has been getting to know him, and he assesses the cultural assets Orlando brings with him to his work.

Winton empathizes with his supervisee and validates his feelings during this rough morning. He then asks Orlando if he would give him some details about how he managed to grow up successfully in his old neighborhood. Winton asks him what he specifically did to resist the seduction of the gangs, what the Brothers and his family said and did that helped and what didn't. "How did they talk to you in ways that made an impact? Were there times that you made some poor judgments? How did you and they handle them? What helped you decide to fight back after your setbacks? What aspects of your culture successfully competed with the lure of gang life?"

Orlando seems to appreciate the genuine interest Winton expresses and he easily reflects on the ways he received help in his neighborhood and how he did and did not use it. At some point, he begins to realize that Winton is using some of the same "strength-based" questions and methods he had been suggesting that Orlando use in relationship building and assessments with his clients. Winton openly confirms this and explains, "Of course I am! These strength-based questions I'm asking aren't just techniques to get information in some abstract way. When I'm asking them, we *both* are reflecting on the resources you have available to you that you (and I) might not be keying into that can help you help your clients. By the way, I've also been using that ethnographic interviewing method we've discussed—not because I just want to demonstrate it to you (although I guess it does that, too), but because it truly helps me find out more about who you are and what you have to offer. In fact, if you find this helpful, I hope you will use these approaches more often with your clients." Orlando smilingly responds, "OK, OK, so how about we continue doing this inventory of my 'cultural assets.' I'm not sure about you, but I was finally beginning to get some ideas here that are helping."

Notice how Winton uses and is explicit about using strength-oriented assessment questions and the ethnographic interviewing method we discuss in Chapter 2; he uses them to focus both himself and Orlando on what can work in this situation. It is easy for Winton, too, to become discouraged about the "battle," and using a strength-based approach, following an appropriate validation of Orlando's feelings and perceptions, shifts the conversation into a direction that is more proactive and helpful for them both.

And for good reason. Reviewing Orlando's cultural assets is not just a technique to help make him feel better or for relationship building or assessment in some abstract sense. Orlando truly has developed survival skills, and utilized religious belief systems and community networks successfully. Punctuating (i.e., highlighting) them unlocks a wealth of experience and ideas he can draw on to help his clients in this situation, mainly because they *have worked*. And they have worked in a way that is authentic to him because it is based on who he is and where he comes from.

That Winton is explicit about using these approaches is genuine and honest, and he is quite open about urging Orlando to try them. Highlighting their efficacy increases the possibility that they can serve as a model Orlando will use with his clients—if he finds it helpful in this situation. (If he or the clients experience them as intrusive, it is, of course, best to back off.) Notice, too, how Winton uses the opportunity to demonstrate the value of these methods in a way that competes with the negative mind-set Orlando has at the beginning of the meeting.

Returning to Lum's model, we see that he goes beyond his definition of assessment and his explanation of "cultural assets," suggesting that clinicians (supervisees) use several specific assessment dimensions to evaluate the client's multicultural attributes. The categories he suggests include biological, psychological, social, cultural, gender, and spiritual dimensions. He tells us that the assessment is intended to illuminate "interactions between the client and the situation" as they relate to information included in these categories (Lum, 2000, p. 329).

Similarly, supervisors can use information that relates to these assessment categories in order to strengthen their assessment of their supervisees, in the spirit of the dual process. For example, with respect to a biological assessment, Lum suggests that the clinician learn about the client's cultural perspectives regarding health. This might be particularly important for the supervisor and supervisee to discuss when they work in health settings or when questions regarding health status are connected to supervisory or clinical situations.

Readers wishing to review these categories further as well as engage in a more complete examination of assessment from a multicultural perspective are urged to review Lum's chapter on assessment (2000, chapter 8). Also, supervisors who are interested in standardized measures to assess supervisees' attitudes, beliefs, and practices are referred to the *Multicultural Awareness, Knowledge, and Skills Survey (MAKSS)* (D'Andrea, Daniels, & Heck, 1991), which can also be utilized to measure levels of desired change in supervisees over time (see Appendix B).

Experience and Development Level

In addition to considering the supervisee's multicultural attributes and cultural assets, it is useful to assess the experience and level of development supervisees bring to their clinical work in terms of their prior knowledge, skills, and professional attitudes. This information mainly helps supervisors formulate the kind and extent of direction they provide. Newer clinicians or clinicians working on methods novel to them generally require greater structure or direction; more experienced clinicians need less. In this section, we briefly review several conceptual models that can help supervisors assess for this information and the implications for their use.

Munson (2002) offers 11 variables that make up what he calls an "educational assessment." Attention to findings from Munson's educational assessment answers his question, "What does the student or new supervisee know as he or she enters the new situation? What does he or she need to learn?" (p. 150). The variables Munson uses to get this information include previous experience, ethical awareness, theoretical knowledge, experience doing assessments and/or diagnosis, intervention skills, organizational understanding, agency functioning, attitudes and values, goals and objectives, previous supervision, and learning impediments (pp. 150–154). (Munson, 2002, pp. 498–502, uses the Educational Assessment Scale (EAS) to organize this educational assessment. It is reprinted in Appendix C and can be a good way to assess these features.)

Haynes, Corey, and Moulton (2003, pp. 112–117) review several developmental models that organize an approach to supervision based on the supervisee's stage of development. These models basically suggest that supervisors vary their approaches as their supervisees develop expertise and confidence over time. Haynes et al. outline the integrated developmental model (IDM) conceptualized by Stoltenberg, McNeil, and Delworth as well as a model developed by Skovholt and Ronnestad. In addition, they offer their own "Blueprint for Developmental Supervision" which describes the kinds of behavior generally expected of supervisors and supervisees at each of three developmental stages. We summarize their model below.

During the first stage of development, Haynes, Corey, and Moulton (2003, pp. 115–116) suggest close monitoring and control on the part of the supervisor as the relationship is developed, competencies are assessed, and education provided. The middle stage involves greater sharing of responsibilities, with some expectation of tension as the supervisee moves from dependent to more independent practice. Finally, the ending stage acknowledges the advanced skills of the supervisee and is geared toward facilitating the move more fully to independent professional practice. The authors caution that the stages should account for individual differences with respect to prior knowledge and skill, and that variations are expected depending on theoretical orientation, type of therapy used, and population served. Appendix D offers a reprint of Haynes, Corey, and Moulton's "Blueprint" for the interested reader.

Bernard and Goodyear (1998, pp. 52–60) provide a detailed and comprehensive review of the empirical literature on developmental differences and feature a section on experience. The authors offer eight guidelines for supervisors to consider with respect to experience (pp. 58–59) that are summarized in outline form below.

1. Bernard and Goodyear assert that experience under supervision is a reliable measure of development. Therefore, supervisors should assume that supervisees with different levels of experience require different kinds of interventions.

2. In their reviews, Bernard and Goodyear observe that supervisees should increasingly exhibit greater self awareness, motivation, consistency, and autonomy as they gain experience. If these features are not forthcoming, they caution, more direction should be instituted and other factors (such as conceptual level) should be considered.

3. They suggest that supervisors concentrate on helping newer supervisees "organize client information into meaningful themes" (p. 58). They suggest that it would be inappropriate to focus on personal issues for the novice unless they are blocked from grasping conceptual information.

4. Bernard and Goodyear make distinctions between newer and more advanced supervisees in terms of flexibility and dominance. They suggest that novice supervisees are more rigid and forceful when providing interventions such as confrontation than are more advanced supervisees. If advanced supervisees are not flexible or are threatened, they may experience a case as beyond their level of competence and may require more direction or attention to personal issues. The authors suggest that supervisees of all experience levels do well with modeling in these circumstances.

5. Role ambiguity is not uncommon for newer supervisees and considerable time should be spent exploring the roles of helper and supervisee. Tension with more advanced supervisees might be an indication of the supervisee's wish for greater autonomy.

6. In most cases, advanced supervisees require and want less structure, and supervision is generally more idiosyncratic than with novices. The authors suggest, however, that under certain circumstances, like a crisis, for instance, or a particularly difficult client, advanced supervisees often welcome greater direction.

7. When supervising novice supervisors, who are supervising novice trainees, the authors suggest that extra attention be given to relationship issues such as self-awareness, because these workers might be distracted by assimilation into new roles and miss nuances in this area. Later in the chapter, they also suggest that newer trainees do best with attention to "universal helping behaviors" (similar to the "core" relationship skills we discuss in Chapter 2) as opposed to highly theoretical information.

8. Bernard and Goodyear suggest that supervision should benefit practitioners throughout their careers and terms such as *advanced* and *expert* should be used carefully because of the limits of current research.

There is some debate in the literature about the efficacy of the current research on developmental models. Bernard and Goodyear caution us "that developmental models are too simplistic to predict trainee behavior in any comprehensive and consistent way" (p. 60). In fact, caution should generally be exercised when making characteristic attributions like "development level" or "learning styles" (discussed next). Global-stable variables such as these mainly provide broad brushstrokes that can help provide a context of understanding (in our case, a basic assessment that informs the supervision process going forward). They can also be misleading, however, unless important situational variables are taken into account and other unique qualities are considered. Having stated these cautions, we turn next to our discussion of learning styles.

Learning Style

Along with knowledge of multicultural attributes, experience, and developmental level, supervisors assess the supervisee's learning style in the context of adult learning theory. This is done to get a picture of how supervisees learn so that supervisors can vary their feedback methods accordingly to maximize professional growth. Because our work has such a strong educational component, and because we work with adults, it makes sense to base our discussion on adult learning theory. Therefore, we briefly outline the latest version of Knowles's classic model on adult learning (Knowles, Holton, & Swanson, 1998) and highlight Kolb's (1984) experiential learning approach as it is featured in the orientation to learning principle of that model.

Adult Learning Knowles et al. (1998) have organized a set of "core adult learning principles that apply to all learning situations" and are easily adapted to fit "the uniqueness of the learner and learning situation" (pp. 2–3). The authors posit the following six learning principles, which fit well in the supervisory setting:

1. *The Need to Know.* Knowles, Holton, and Swanson suggest that adults need to understand the value of learning something before undertaking to learn it. Most supervisees easily see the general value of learning new information and skills in the context of clinical supervision; however, they may resist learning new methods or participating in new experiences unless they see the benefits of doing so. For example, in the case of Sam and Dave, Dave clearly knows the benefits of reviewing videotape and Sam didn't have to make a case for the efficacy of that learning experience. In the last case example, Winton explains and demonstrates the usefulness of ethnographic interviewing and strength-based questions, even though he, too, was not pressed for an explanation. "The need to know" may require more attention depending on the particular supervisee and other variables discussed below.

In those cases, supervisors would do well to have a clear rationale for suggested learning experiences and be prepared to explain them.

2. *The Learners' Self-Concept.* The authors assume that adults see themselves as responsible for their own decisions and basically need to be seen and treated as capable of self-direction. They may resist situations in which they feel their independence is challenged. This is not unlike the tension Haynes et al. (2003) predict in the middle stage of their "Blueprint for Developmental Supervision" where there is a "transition from dependency to independent practice" (see Appendix D). Mindful of the importance of the learner's self-concept, they suggest methods that facilitate increased sharing of responsibilities with heavy emphasis on collaborative approaches.

3. *The Role of the Learners' Experiences.* As we specifically discuss in this chapter, and assume throughout the book, supervisees enter supervision with a wide range of personal, multicultural, and professional experiences. Assessing for these supports the authors' suggestion that such assessment be used to individualize teaching and learning activities. Knowles and colleagues (1998) point out that the "richest resources for learning reside in the adult learners themselves" and that experiential techniques (so prevalent in the supervision setting: direct observation of work with clients, role playing, group supervision) nicely tap into the learners' personal resources.

   The authors also show that in many ways, adults equate who they are with their experiences, and ignoring or devaluing these can be perceived as rejecting them as persons. As we discuss in the context of caring confrontations, it can be tricky to accept and value the person while at the same time challenging certain ways of thinking and behaving in support of growth.

4. *Readiness to Learn.* There is a progression of things adults need to know to manage life's tasks effectively. In our context, the relevance of this principle is related to the importance of assessing supervisee readiness as supervisees move through various stages of their professional development. For example, thoughtful supervisors try to time the assignment of increasingly challenging case situations to coordinate with increases in the supervisee's knowledge, skills, and professional attitudes and values.

5. *Motivation.* The authors say that while adults are responsive to external motivators (promotions, graduate degrees, licensing in our situation), internal pressures such as self-esteem or satisfaction on the job can be more powerful. Therefore, assessing and learning what is internally satisfying for the supervisee can cue the supervisor to provide the kind of learning opportunities that help sustain motivation for continued growth.

6. *Orientation to Learning.* In contrast to a "subject" orientation used to teach children and youth in most schools, Knowles et al. (1998) suggest that adults learn best when opportunities for learning are presented in connection to real-life situations. They refer to Kolb's (1984) leadership in promulgating the use of "experiential learning" in this regard. We focus on Kolb's work directly at this point in the text because of the efficacy of his

work as applied to supervision. Readers wishing to learn more about the six principles of adult learning (known more technically as "Androgogy"), should consult Knowles et al. (1998, chapters 4 & 7).

Experiential Learning Kolb defines experiential learning as "the process whereby knowledge is created through the transformation of experience" (1984, p. 38). He discusses this way of understanding the world as a "holistic integrative perspective on learning that combines experience, perception, cognition, and behavior" (p. 21). His theory is built on the premise that there are four kinds of abilities people can use to "transform their experience" and achieve new "knowledge, skills, or attitudes" (p. 30).

People tend to use one or several of these abilities in combination to transform experience into learning. It is helpful to key in on those abilities that resonate most for particular supervisees in our assessment so that we can create teaching strategies structured to maximize their learning. We summarize Kolb's (1984, p. 30) four abilities and briefly consider implications for supervision:

- Concrete experience (CE). This is an ability that allows individuals "to involve themselves fully, openly, and without bias in new experiences" (p. 30). This kind of ability is reflected in learning by doing. Learning may be facilitated best through direct experiences with clients and simulations like behavior rehearsal (role play).

- Reflective observation (RO). This ability allows for reflection and observation of experiences from many perspectives. Supervisees who are strong in this area learn well through observing others and also by discussions in individual and group supervision.

- Abstract conceptualization (AC). This ability allows for creation of concepts "that integrate . . . observations into logically sound theories" (p. 30). It reflects learning through a kind of abstract reasoning that may be facilitated by allowing for time to consider and integrate information.

- Active experimentation (AE). This is an action-oriented ability that allows the supervisee to "use . . . theories to make decisions and solve problems" (p. 30). Knowles et al. interpret this as an ability to test implications of new concepts in new situations (p. 147). Strategies for learning may involve behavior rehearsal and opportunities to play out ideas as opposed to a more abstract format.

These abilities are not discrete from one another although Kolb suggests that people emphasize certain of these abilities over others "as a result of our hereditary equipment, our particular past life experience, and the demands of our present environment" (1984, p. 76). Kolb's research further led him to conceptualize four learning styles that reflect unique combinations of the learning abilities discussed above based on empirical findings from an instrument he developed, the *Learning Style Inventory* (Kolb, 1976).

For a more in-depth analysis of these styles, the interested reader is referred to Kolb (1984, pp. 61–98). Bernard and Goodyear (1998, pp. 36–37) provide a shorter overview of these styles and review applications to the supervision of childcare workers. They also summarize the Myers–Briggs Type Indicator (Myers, 1962; Myers & McCaulley, 1985) for readers who wish to learn more about the implications of particular cognitive styles for supervision.

DIRECT AND INDIRECT METHODS
OF ASSESSMENT

A thorough assessment of the supervisee's actual clinical work is as important for the supervisory process as a thorough assessment of the client is for the therapeutic process. The topography is different, of course, but the mind-set supervisors use as they enter into the assessment process is similar, in the spirit of the dual process. They both want to learn about the problems and strengths of their clients or supervisees given who they are and the contract that has determined the purposes for meeting.

In this next section of the chapter, we discuss the discovery function of assessment as conducted through the use of both direct and indirect methods. Supervisors assess the supervisee's direct clinical work and seek to discover their problems and strengths in a context that is informed by a growing understanding of their multicultural attributes, experience, and developmental level as well as their learning styles (as discussed in the last section). When we assess for problems, we more or less mean areas targeted for growth. We use the term *problems* interchangeably with the terms *challenges* and *limitations*. The term *strengths* is used interchangeably with the term *competencies* to denote some kind of expertise.

Audio- and videotaping, live observation, and live supervision are direct methods of assessment discussed in the first part of the section. These techniques allow for electronic and/or actual observation of interactions between the supervisee and the client. Indirect methods of assessment rely on the supervisor's ability to make inferences about supervisee/client interaction based on verbal or written information about case material supplied by the supervisee. These include verbal reports, process recording, and case study review. Our review of indirect assessment methods concludes this chapter. We continue our discussion of the work phase in the next chapter by discussing how problems and strengths are conceptualized into themes that are periodically summarized in the formative assessment. These themes also form the basis of goals for growth and revision of the supervisory contract.

Direct Methods of Assessment

Audio- and Videotape   Audio- and videotaping are two methods that allow the supervisor to observe the supervisee's work with clients directly, an advantage in that the supervisor has accurate information regarding the therapeutic interaction. Having obtained written consent to tape part or all of a session with a client, the supervisory pair has several options for how the tape can be used to discover problems and strengths (as the basis for feedback).

The supervisor can listen to or watch all or part of the tape and provide a written or verbal review for the supervisee. This method may be time consuming and leaves out the possibility of immediate interaction with the supervisee, but because there are no interruptions, there may be greater opportunity for continuity in the assessment and feedback. As in the case of Sam and Dave, supervisees can review their tapes privately at their own pace, play selected parts for the supervisor, and come prepared with questions and observations of their own. In both cases, supervisors have the option of picking out particular interactions and key in on them in order to share observations about problems and strengths for assessment or intervention.

Supervisees who have not had the opportunity to use tape are sometimes reticent to take advantage of this modality at first because they are self-conscious or fear being criticized for making mistakes in so public a forum (the same is obviously true for live observation and supervision). The establishment of a safe and trusting relationship utilizing the skills and attributes previously discussed can pay great dividends at moments like this. The existence of a supportive atmosphere can help supervisees until they become more comfortable and desensitized to the process. Normalizing mistakes can also be particularly helpful in reducing anxiety and defensiveness. Munson (2002, p. 241) refers to this process as "error acceptance learning." He says that

> errors in practice are expected and known to occur, and the supervision process will be a search for such errors without punitive action for the errors discovered. This is similar to the Airline Pilot Association's policy of encouraging pilots to report near misses and other pilot errors without penalty so they can be studied and ways found to remedy them. This mode of evaluation is aimed more at helping the client than it is at judging the practitioner. (pp. 241–242)

Even if successful in providing a safe, nonjudgmental, error accepting, "powering with" atmosphere, some supervisees become so uncomfortable with taping and other methods of direct assessment that it actively interferes with their work. Using small bits of tape, chosen by the supervisee, may facilitate a desensitization process. Renowned family therapist and supervisor Jay Haley suggests that supervisors instruct anxious supervisees to choose a piece of videotape for review and regardless of their true self-evaluation state that it is their *worst* work. The supervisor "assumes the same" out loud in order to take off pressure to perform and then invites the supervisee to the business of working with the specific strengths and limitations observed (personal communication, October, 1991).

Some clients may experience similar discomfort with direct observation even though they may initially consent to it. Discontinuing direct observation is the simple and ethical choice in such instances (many clients actually appreciate taping and live approaches, understanding that supervisors are available to provide additional input and help). Should supervisors reach an end point in their attempts to facilitate an environment safe enough for the supervisee and client, they must rely on other assessment methods.

Live Observation and Supervision Similar to taping, live observation and supervision are methods of direct assessment (and sometimes, intervention) that allow the supervisor a more complete impression of the relationship between the client and the supervisee. Supervisors can observe a live session by sitting in on a session or by watching behind a one-way mirror. Because the supervisor is watching the interaction, both the supervisee and the client have help nearby in terms of immediate availability in case of an emergency.

Live supervision takes live observation a step further because the supervisor both observes *and participates* in the session with the client and the supervisee. Live supervision can be utilized with the supervisee and an individual supervisor or with a team; it can combine elements of both assessment and intervention. Bernard and Goodyear (1998) provide an excellent review of Bubenzer, Mahrle, and West's list of six methods used to conduct live supervision: bug in the ear, monitoring, in vivo, walk-in, phone in, and consultation breaks; they also discuss Klitzke and Lombardo's bug in the eye. In addition, they detail a comprehensive literature review complete with a section on advantages and disadvantages of each (pp. 132–142). We summarize their review below:

1. *Bug-in-the-ear or "BITE."* The supervisee wears an earphone and the supervisor, who is sitting observing the supervisee and client from behind a one-way mirror, offers suggestions during the session. This technique is helpful for inexperienced supervisees who can benefit from direct coaching and immediate reinforcement. The downside is that the incoming information may be distracting because it is being received while the therapy is in session and might also encourage dependence on the information flow for the supervisee.

2. *Monitoring.* This technique requires the supervisor to monitor the session between the supervisee and client from the observation room and then enter the therapy room to intervene directly in the session. If done with sensitivity and with the dual process in mind, this method can provide an excellent opportunity to model an appropriate intervention. As an invited consultant, at the request of more experienced therapists, there may be a special opportunity to enter the therapy and break an impasse in the treatment.

3. *"In Vivo."* Similar to monitoring, the supervisor enters the therapy room, but instead of intervening directly, consults with the supervisee in front of the client. As Bernard and Goodyear suggest, this supervision can also be used as a kind of intervention "by heightening the family's awareness of particular dynamics, especially when dynamics are therapeutically reframed for the benefit of the family" (1998, p. 133). It is similar to an open consultation when used with a reflecting team (these methods are discussed in the next section).

4. *Walk-in.* Similar to the previous two methods, the walk-in involves a supervisor who enters the session "at some deliberate moment, interacts with both the therapist and the clients, and then leaves" (Bernard & Goodyear, 1998, p. 133). Bernard and Goodyear suggest that this method

"does not imply an emergency, nor does it imply the kind of collegiality that is evident with in vivo supervision" (p. 133).

5. *Phone-ins and consultation breaks.* Both of these methods interrupt therapy either by a phone-in from the supervisor behind the one-way mirror or by the therapist leaving the room at the sound of a signal from the supervisor for a consultation break. Both are quite common and provide immediate information. The phone-in can be a quick way to give feedback whereas the consultation break can provide an opportunity to exchange information outside the presence of the client.

6. *Bug-in-the-eye.* Similar to the use of a TelePrompTer, this method requires the supervisor to type in suggestions on a keyboard from the observation room; these are subsequently displayed on a monitor behind the client. The supervisee chooses the moment to read the message, thereby retaining control over the timing of the reception unlike the BITE. In addition, the feedback comments can be stored on disk for later discussion in supervision.

Live supervision may also be conducted in a team supervision format with or without an identified leader. For example, a team may be led by a primary supervisor who is in charge, or a group may be set up without a designated leader for the purposes of peer supervision. Group members in both formats take a more or less active role in the feedback process depending upon the setting, level of experience, style or role of a designated supervisor, and so on.

Many of the same live supervision techniques referred to earlier are also utilized to assess and provide feedback in the live team setting. One such method, for example, parallels the in vivo technique mentioned above. It is referred to as the reflecting team approach (Anderson, 1987) and is widely utilized among family therapists (where live supervision got its start). Families watch as the observing reflecting team participates in an open consultation about their case. Not only can this be an effective mode of assessment, but it can also generate creative interventions that reflect the synergistic energies of the team.

Utilizing live team approaches can be quite challenging. Munson (2002) advises, "Live supervision is more than supervision—it is teamwork that requires much role flexibility, role acceptance, and role confidence on the part of the supervisor. When live supervision is used, the supervisor has to be more responsible and aware than is the case in other forms of supervision" (p. 371). He cautions that supervising a team essentially requires many of the skills of a group leader and supervisor *plus* on-the-spot responsibility for the welfare of the client. For a more in-depth account of the literature reviewing team supervision including advantages and disadvantages, the reader is referred to Bernard and Goodyear (1998, pp. 141–148).

Indirect Methods of Assessment

Indirect methods of assessment do not involve direct observation of the supervisee/client interaction. Information about problems and strengths in the work phase is discovered by making inferences from what supervisees say (e.g., verbal report) or write (e.g., process recordings or case studies), as they report on their clinical work. This format is referred to as self-report, case review, or case consultation and often centers on case material related to the clients with whom the supervisee works. Supervisors can focus their attention and the ensuing discussion in ways that depend on the supervisee's learning objectives and responsibilities specified in the supervisory contract, needs of the client, and requirements of the agency. The framework we suggest here is informed by Munson (2002) and McCollum and Wetchler (1995) and their views on how indirect methods can be used.

Verbal Report   Munson (2002, p. 154) sees verbal report regarding "case material as the foundation of supervisory clinical techniques," and he provides a list of 10 questions that may be used by the supervisor to help learn about the clinical interaction. He asks about the supervisee's thoughts and feelings regarding the client, perceptions about the client's thoughts and feelings, the theoretical basis for interventions, goals, and concerns about practice, and so on. He believes that questions along this line of thinking reveal "the essence of the treatment relationship" (p. 155).

McCollum and Wetchler (1995) believe that "to be useful, case consultation must be more than just 'talking about clients' " (p. 157). They suggest that supervisors can use case consultation best by examining four areas with their supervisees in the context of their ongoing verbal reports:

> (a) understanding the "architecture" of the therapy process (in essence, the broad picture of how the supervisee works with the client over time and conceptualizes the therapy process into a coherent whole), (b) helping trainees build theoretical models of change, (c) understanding the clients' broader context, i.e., the larger systems to which the client relates,
> (d) understanding the therapist's broader context, e.g., the work environment, family of origin issues, multicultural issues, etc. (p. 157)

Process Recording   In addition to verbal report, supervisors can discover problems and strengths related to goals and responsibilities in the supervisory contract through the use of a written medium. One method is the process recording. A process recording is essentially a transcript of the proceedings between supervisee and client as remembered by the supervisee. The supervisee recounts and summarizes the actual conversation then records thoughts, feelings, and impressions in relation to the interactions reviewed. (This process is called a *verbatim* in clinical pastoral education, and it is an assessment instrument used in clinical pastoral education (C.P.E.) training programs. It is also similar to interpersonal process recall (IPR) (Kagen & Kagen, 1997).

The process recording is one way for supervisors to learn what has taken place in a session and train supervisees to reflect on their feelings and thoughts about the clinical interaction. A limitation is that supervisees may forget key interactions or simply avoid writing about what they think are mistakes. In addition, process recordings may be time consuming to write as well as to review. For these reasons, other methods of assessment are often utilized instead of or in addition to process recordings.

Case Study Review Unlike process recordings, case studies are more a written conceptualization of a case than a transcription. (This is a particular favorite for supervisees whose learning styles, as discussed in the first part of this chapter, are oriented to reflective observation, abstract conceptualization, or some combination of both.) Typically, the supervisee evaluates a case for review according to several pertinent variables, including these:

1. Presenting problem or concern (using the words and concepts of the client(s))
2. (Supervisee's) conceptualization of problems and/or needs
3. Goals of intervention and criteria for success
4. Strengths of the client. (How the client has shown some success in relation to the problem in the past, i.e., personal resources including pertinent cultural assets)
5. Interventions chosen
6. Current disposition of the case

Case studies give the supervisee an opportunity to pull together a lot of potentially complicated information in a format that conceptually reflects the clinical process. The supervisory pair may then take the opportunity to work, that is, build knowledge, skills, and professional attitudes and values using the material in the case as a reference point. Consideration of case studies, like other indirect methods of case consultation, have an advantage in their "ability to examine larger context issues, and provide time for reflection" (McCollum & Wetchler, 1995, p. 164). (The case study format can also serve as the basis of an initial diagnostic assessment; I have worked with several agencies that have adapted and adopted this essentially strength-based format.)

There are inherent challenges in the discovery of the supervisee's problems and strengths when using indirect methods. The degree to which the supervisor can gain accurate information about the actual supervisee/client interaction is limited, as is the opportunity to respond with immediacy if desired. In actuality, direct and indirect discovery formats complement each other, and in many ways they offset the disadvantages each presents when used alone. Therefore, it is advisable to use a judicious combination of both.

In the next chapter, we see how the information discovered by these methods is conceptualized into themes organized around problems and strengths in the formative assessment. These themes serve as the basis for establishing goals for growth and subsequent revision of the supervisory contract. Although we do not focus on the supervisor's role as manager and the supervisee's role as staff member in this chapter, the manager assesses for problems and strengths administratively as well as clinically. Subsequent goals for growth, action plans, and criteria for success are also determined with respect to administrative responsibilities.

5

𝕍𝔈

Formative Assessment, Goals for Growth, and Contract Revision

With a shift from engagement to the work phase, greater attention is given to the supervisee's work directly with clients as it relates to the clinical responsibilities and learning objectives agreed to in the supervisory contract. The supervisor as manager also assesses the supervisee/ staff member's performance with respect to the individual's administrative responsibilities. In the previous chapter, we discussed direct and indirect methods that are used to assess supervisees' problems and strengths in light of their multicultural attributes, developmental level, experience, and learning styles. This, of course, is accomplished in a context where the supervisory relationship continues to develop.

As supervisors learn more about the supervisee's clinical work (and administrative work), it is important to conceptualize problems and strengths discovered from the assessment and communicate these observations directly to the supervisee. We define this feedback as a communication of observations between supervisor and supervisee, and for our purposes here, we use the term in two ways. First, *direct feedback* can be provided immediately as a form of intervention that relates to specific observations in specific instances. Or it can be given more generally, as a *summary* of trends or themes in the supervisee's work that are observed over time.

We begin this chapter with a discussion of the latter, a kind of summary known as a *formative assessment*, which includes both the conceptualization of themes or trends related to problems and strengths and communication about those observations with the supervisee. Giving immediate feedback in specific instances, referred to here as direct feedback, is technically a kind of intervention that we refer to throughout the book and discuss more fully in the next chapter.

Armed with greater understanding of their work from the formative assessment, supervisees can join with their supervisors to create specific and informed choices about goals for growth, action plans and criteria for future success. As goals for growth that relate to clinical (and/or administrative) responsibilities are identified, it is important to revise the supervisory contract so that it reflects these changes or modifications in learning objectives and expectations for service.

We explore these processes in the second and third sections of the chapter as they set the stage for the discussion of intervention in the work phase in Chapters 6 and 7.

THE FORMATIVE ASSESSMENT

The formative assessment is a kind of summary review of the supervisee's strengths and problems over time as conceptualized by the supervisor in collaboration with the supervisee. This conceptualization organizes observations about trends in the supervisee's work into themes referred to here as "themes organized around problems" and/or "themes organized around strengths." Various types of the formative assessment are referred to in the literature as *formative feedback* or *formative evaluation* and these terms are often used interchangeably (Bernard & Goodyear, 1998; Falvey, 2002; Levy, 1983; Robiner, Fuhrman, & Bobbitt, 1990; Robiner, Fuhrman, & Risvedt, 1993; Shulman, 1993). A distinction is generally made between the formative assessment, which is considered to be informal and used mainly for educative purposes and the *summative evaluation*. The summative evaluation is a more formal, periodic evaluation that has a stronger emphasis on accountability. (We consider the summative evaluation in Chapter 7 in the context of interventions related to the managerial/administrative role of the supervisor.)

The first task of the supervisor in conducting a formative assessment is to conceptualize information discovered from direct and indirect assessments of the supervisee's work into the aforementioned themes. These themes are best organized to focus on effective work (strengths) as well as spell out areas that require growth (problems). The second task is to discuss these themes with the supervisee in order to create goals for growth, action plans, and criteria for success that adjust, add to, or replace learning objectives and expectations in a revised supervisory contract (discussed later in the chapter).

Conceptualizing and communicating information learned from assessment into themes is not a one-way street, with the supervisor making an objective diagnosis about problems or deficits and recommending the proper "treatment"—a pattern similar to the medical model. (The interested reader is referred to an excellent review of the medical model as a paradigm for the helping professions offered by De Jong & Berg, 2002, pp. 6–8.) Rather, recent trends in clinical work and supervision describe a more inclusive, less hierarchical, strength-based framework for practice that emphasizes competence (similar to the cultural assets described in the last chapter). Clients and supervisees are invited to collaborate in conceptualizing and defining problems using a future orientation that concentrates on solutions. To learn more about approaches that subscribe to this point of view, readers may review the following: a strengths perspective (Saleebey, 1992; Lum, 2000); a solution-focused approach (de Shazer, 1985; De Jong & Miller, 1995); a solution-building approach (De Jong & Berg, 2002); a narrative approach (White & Epston, 1990); and a review of perspectives like these in the context of supervision (Edwards & Chen, 1999).

Clinician and client (or supervisor and supervisee) collaborate on an understanding of problems together and then co-construct or build solutions that empower clients and supervisees to draw on the many resources they have available to them. This collaboration *does not eliminate* the validity of the supervisor's expertise. The supervisor's perspective in regard to themes around problems and strengths is and will always be central to the process as we discuss it here. Collaboration however, allows a broader perspective than only the supervisor's take or construction of reality—which is not the only or *necessarily* the best one.

Edwards and Chen (1999) favor a similar approach to supervision in that "there exists a give and take, where the supervisor does not assume to have a more correct or privileged knowledge of both the supervisee's and clients' goals, intentions, or views, and where the supervisor works intentionally to create a strength-based supervision" (pp. 351–353). While essentially espousing a strength-based orientation, they too acknowledge the importance of the supervisor's point of view. They cite Atkinson and Heath in this regard and apply their comments about a comparable family therapy approach to supervision:

> Family therapists will continually recognize and acknowledge that their views are not objective or "true" in any determinable way, but rather, that they are constructed from the limited (but important) viewpoint of the therapist, and that clients should feel free to disagree. However . . . therapists will recognize that their ideas and suggestions may be helpful if heard, and they will not hesitate to share them. (p. 350)

Edwards and Chen's give and take is consistent with the model of supervision we discuss here in that it values the perceptions of the supervisee (the use of their term *co-vision* is particularly appealing) and focuses on strengths. At the same time, the importance of the supervisor's viewpoint in conceptualizing both strengths *and* problems and the *responsibility* to communicate with the supervisee about those observations cannot be overstated. We focus our attention next on the conceptualization and communication of themes organized around strengths.

Themes Organized Around Strengths

Conceptualization and feedback on strengths is of major importance in the formative assessment and is all too frequently underutilized and underestimated as a powerful supervision tool. Focusing on competent behavior raises the probability that supervisees will "do more of it" as they come to understand what is effective. The chance that effective behavior will transfer and generalize is also increased, and that safety and trust in the relationship will be sustained as attention to success forms the foundation for future growth possibilities. When the supervisory pair spends time reviewing positive attributes and behavior, both supervisor and supervisee are reminded of what the supervisee has to offer. Communications like this can also soften the emotional tone of the relationship if there has previously been too much emphasis on problems.

Effective supervisors conceptualize and share their own observations about the strengths that they see in their supervisee's work. They also utilize a variety of strength-based techniques to help supervisees consider their own work in novel ways, so that the supervisees can discover and reflect on their own resources and competence. Supervisors can ask supervisees to consider *how* they reached an effective intervention, rather than stop at mutual recognition. (I often say to supervisees—and supervisors—whom I supervise that the second remark following an effective behavior choice is "Good job." The first is "How did you accomplish that?")

Asking, for example, "What made you decide to use a caring confrontation in that instance?" sparks a dialogue that goes beyond what the supervisor alone could imagine and stimulates a reflection by the supervisee that often yields insight surprising to them both. This process and the insights it reveals, although discussed here in the context of formative assessments, is *simultaneously an intervention* designed to facilitate professional growth (we discuss this further in Chapter 6). Similar techniques such as the use of coping and scaling questions (discussed in the next section) as well as exploration for exceptions (De Jong & Miller, 1995; De Jong & Berg, 2002) are strength-based interviewing techniques that are easily adapted for supervision (and are also forms of assessment that may be considered interventions).

Themes Organized Around Problems

Conceptualization of problems in the formative assessment alerts the supervisory pair to areas in need of growth. Supervisees learn where they stand and can then remove obstacles to further growth as they and their supervisors co-construct new possibilities and more effective approaches to practice. We carry through our discussion of Lum's practice process stages in this regard.

Lum's Process Stage Approach: Problem Identification
Lum (2000) advocates a nonpathological view of problems that is consistent with the approach we have been discussing here. He suggests a creative way to identify problems: "Rather than trying to uncover the dysfunctional aspect of a problem, the worker interprets the problem as symptomatic of a positive striving

that has been hindered by an obstacle in the client's [or in our case the super-visee's professional] life" (p. 134). Lum says that "learning" and "focusing" are the tasks of the problem identification stage. Notice the collaborative style he articulates as he describes the meaning and use of these concepts:

> Learning consists of uncovering essential problem themes and then detailing them with facts. Focusing occurs when the worker and client decide to settle on a particular problem that both parties consider primary. As the worker probes and the client responds, both learn about dimensions of the problem. The worker describes the problem as a logical sequence of events on the basis of information supplied by the client. The client gains new insights into the problem. Which segment of the problem seems most manageable to the worker and client? What portion of the problem can most readily be detailed, studied, and analyzed? What is the sequence or pattern of problem events? . . . Problem identification moves from general learning about problem issues to focusing on a specific problem. (p. 135)

His concepts about problem identification, learning, and focusing are well applied to the context of supervision. The supervisor makes observations on the basis of information garnered from the assessment process and the super-visee is respectfully invited to participate in problem identification. The likeli-hood of defensiveness in the supervisee is reduced with this collaborative approach; and as Lum suggests, clients (supervisees) become ready to share information about problems once they believe that they will not be shamed in the disclosure.

Returning to the conceptualization of and communication about problems and strengths, note that the timing and predictability of formative assessments is also important. When formative assessments are considered a normal part of their experience, done in a regular and timely fashion, supervisees build them into their expectations and are prepared for them psychologically. Evaluation and self-evaluation become "just an expected part of the process," and they (and their supervisors!) become desensitized to a process that can be quite uncomfortable if done sporadically or only in a crisis. Regular formative assess-ments also serve as a respectful way to prepare the supervisee for more formal summative evaluations often required for agency reviews, credentialing pur-poses, licensing, and similar purposes.

Middleman and Rhodes (cited in Bernard and Goodyear, 1998, p. 160) believe "that formative evaluation [should] occur often enough for changes to be suggested with time to implement them before the summative evaluation. In other words, evaluation should be dynamic and relevant throughout the supervision experience, not just at the beginning and end." Bernard and Goodyear add that "the time when the absence of such a dynamic process becomes a conspicuous issue is in the unfortunate circumstance of a negative final evaluation" and that "the time to consider this unfortunate possibility is in the beginning of the evaluative process, not at the end" (p. 160).

Armed with knowledge about themes organized around strengths and problems from formative assessments, supervisors and supervisees can make specific and informed choices about what to do with this information. The following section addresses the next step in the work phase: setting goals for growth, devising action plans, and developing criteria for determining success. Expectations for learning and service can then be adjusted and reflected in the revised supervisory contract.

GOALS FOR GROWTH, ACTION PLANS, AND CRITERIA FOR SUCCESS

As supervisees continue to work with clients and do formative assessments with their supervisors, attention is given to conceptualizing and communicating about themes organized around their problems and strengths. Supervisors and supervisees begin to co-create goals for growth that relate to these themes and they decide on action plans and criteria for success. The term *goals for growth* means what it describes: desired outcomes for change or professional growth with respect to knowledge, skills, and/or professional attitudes that relate to clinical (and/or administrative responsibilities). *Action plans* are the steps that will be taken to build on strengths, remove obstacles to growth, or remediate problems. *Criteria for success* describe the observed changes that signal success in achieving the goals for growth. The goals for growth seek to build on strengths as well as remediate problems related to clinical and administrative responsibilities in the supervisory contract.

Using Lum's suggestions for "learning" and "focusing" in the identification of problems, it becomes a relatively straightforward process to specify goals for growth, action plans, and criteria for success that are based on Edwards and Chen's (1999) co-vision of supervisee and supervisor. Goals, plans, and criteria with respect to competencies are just as important as those that relate to problems and can be geared to an *extension* of what works.

In developing these goals, plans, and criteria from a strength-based perspective, supervisors might consider the use of "scaling questions" (De Jong & Berg, 2002; De Jong & Miller, 1995). Originally designed to help clients actively reflect and build on effective behavior, this strength-based questioning technique can be adapted to help co-create goals for growth in supervision. For example, the supervisor might ask the supervisee to rate the effectiveness of a particular approach on a scale from 1 to 10 (10 being most effective). If the supervisee rates the outcome at say, 5, the supervisor might ask what would make it an 8 or a 9. This might be construed as a goal for growth to aim for. And if it were an 8 or 9, how would we know it? What would you have to do to reach it? What are the criteria for success?

A case illustration can clarify this discussion on goals for growth and some of the other applicable constructs. Consider the case of Chantey and Billy.

Chantey has just been promoted to supervise a team of three Workforce staff members who work with youth in the inner city. She herself had been a Workforce counselor at one time, so she knows what the job requires. She doesn't quite know, however, what her supervisees require. This is her first experience as a supervisor. She makes herself available every day to each of the workers in a daily review and the focus of discussion usually centers on the needs of the adolescents with whom they work. This parallels the supervision she received, which worked well for her, and in fact works well for two of her three supervisees. They, like she, are well organized, extremely conscientious about following up with their clients, and often cover for each other when there is a time crunch.

Billy, one of two male workers, is another story. Although he connects well with clients, he is regularly late for meetings with them as well as with staff and rarely makes himself available to cover. One might say he violates provisions of the work contract as well as the psychological contract. Chantey has spoken with him about both problems several times. She reports to her supervisor that "nothing sticks. He shapes up for a while, but quickly returns to his old ways. He's got an attitude problem and I just think we should fire him. The new counselors see his behavior, and I worry that they will catch his bad habits."

Leslie, Chantey's supervisor, is an experienced supervisor but fairly new to the agency; they have met with each other only four times in this her first month. But already they have engaged extremely well and Chantey feels safe and trusting in the relationship. Leslie has recently begun to discuss her framework for practice (the one suggested in this book) as a way to help Chantey start organizing her thoughts about Billy and the supervision. From her ongoing assessment of Chantey, Leslie understands that she is a novice supervisor and she makes suggestions that are directive, task specific, and structured, using her understanding of the role of experience and development to help guide her approach. (She also explains the reasons for her suggestions, directed at the adult learner's "need to know.") Leslie suggests that Chantey do the same with Billy and be directive, task specific and structured, realizing that Billy is a newer counselor with little experience.

One of Leslie's early suggestions is for Chantey to set up regular, individual supervision meetings with Billy. As Chantey has been supervising him for several months, it would be a good time to have a review meeting to make sure they are in agreement with respect to the learning objectives, and clinical and administrative responsibilities contained in his supervisory contract. It would also be a good time to prepare a formative assessment and discuss his strengths and limitations from her perspective. (Leslie explains what the formative assessment is and suggests that Chantey also explain it to Billy.)

To prepare for this meeting, Leslie helps Chantey conceptualize Billy's strengths as well as his problems. Because of her strong feelings about his problems, Chantey has given little attention to his strengths. As she and Leslie begin to discuss his ability to relate to his teenage clients and the cultural assets he brings to the agency, they both begin to notice a kind of softening in Chantey's demeanor. Leslie mentions that to her and talks about the value of noting the ways Billy is effective. They also discuss methods that Chantey can use to build on her observations of his good service, and Leslie teaches her how to use some strength-based questions in this regard.

Given Chantey's observations about Billy's problems with lateness and coverage, she suggests that Chantey focus on these issues as "problem themes" in the formative assessment and relate them to the specific administrative expectations for service in the supervisory contract. Leslie recommends that Chantey use a "caring confrontation" with Billy about these problems and discusses this technique with her ("I notice that . . . What is your perspective . . .?).

Assuming that there is some agreement between Chantey and Billy about Billy's problems (Chantey has kept excellent time logs), Leslie suggests that Chantey ask Billy what *he* thinks are appropriate goals for growth, action plans, and criteria for success: "What will you do to change?" "What behavior and attitudes will tell us that you have successfully made changes?" In subsequent meetings, Chantey will give him direct feedback as they track his progress. Progress will be based on the criteria for success to which they both agree and have included as part of their revised supervisory contract. Leslie and Chantey end the meeting discussing the summative evaluation that is due in six months; this evaluation should be a summary of *several* formative assessments and should, therefore, contain no surprises.

This case study illustrates several of the concepts we have been discussing. Leslie helps Chantey create an organizing framework for supervision; she focuses on the initial contract and role induction to start (in both her and Chantey's supervisory relationships). She also moves fairly quickly to an account of Chantey's concerns about her work with Billy because that is where *Chantey's* focus is. She suggests that Chantey use a caring confrontation with Billy that relates to his chronic lateness with clients and staff. Chantey must be clear about her rationale for conceptualizing this as a problem theme as she communicates with Billy using Lum's learning and focusing techniques described in the last section.

Having established that this is indeed a problem that needs remediation, Chantey and Billy can begin to co-create a goal for growth by having Billy tell what *he thinks* the goal should be. Utilizing a strength-based orientation, Chantey can then develop this goal for growth in collaboration with him. They decide on the action steps he will take to remediate the problems and they then focus on the criteria that will show them that Billy is successful. This is the behavior that will tell them he has successfully dealt with lateness in a way that works for his clients, his fellow staff, and for *him*. The direction is set for intervention. They both work to track any instances that reflect successful change and focus on removing any obstacles to growth.

REVISING THE SUPERVISORY CONTRACT

Revising the supervisory contract is a dynamic process and contracts are typically renegotiated and reworked periodically for a variety of reasons. Revisions occur because goals for growth change as problems and strengths develop and are identified during formative assessment. Contracts are also revised as supervisees reach an agreed-on level of success related to goals *previously* requiring growth or when learning objectives have been achieved or new ones developed.

Revisions add to, modify, or inform learning objectives in the initial supervisory contract. For example, Sam and Dave agree to add a goal for growth to Sam's contract that states, "Sam will learn more about how to ask strength-based questions and successfully use this knowledge in family therapy." To attain this goal, Sam makes an action plan to read excerpts from *Interviewing for Solutions* (De Jong & Berg, 2002) and several pertinent journal articles. He also agrees to practice these methods in family therapy and review his work in supervision. Criteria for success will be proper use of these strength-based questions as assessed in supervision through tapes, self-report, and other methods.

Other revisions in the contract may be generated simply by a supervisee's wish to learn new approaches that simply extend his or her knowledge, skills, professional attitudes, and values. For example, supervisees (or their supervisors) may suggest specific goals for growth that will help them to know more about a variety of theories and/or empirical approaches to therapy or to learn skills related to a creative application of their knowledge base that they can use to help clients in their clinical work. Consider this case illustration.

Tim and his supervisor, Lana, decide as a session goal to review a case Tim is working on and conceptualize dynamics of the case from a cognitive behavioral perspective. This relates to one of Tim's learning objectives to "know more" about this perspective. It is clear that Tim already has a fair degree of knowledge about these approaches and Lana asks him if he can see ways to build on the success of this learning objective. They collaborate and together modify his contract to include a new goal for growth: to be able to do effective cognitive behavioral interventions as they relate to the skills for daily living required by his clients.

Lana and Tim work with clients who can appropriately benefit directly from these approaches and Tim takes responsibility to *apply* his cognitive behavioral knowledge in his clinical work as part of his action plan. Success is to be measured by the appropriate use of this perspective as described through verbal report in supervisory sessions and observed during live supervision. Future session goals will change, in turn, to reflect the latest renegotiation of his supervisory contract.

Lana and Tim utilize a kind of co-vision to build on his strengths with a goal for growth: that he apply his knowledge and do cognitive behavioral interventions that relate to the skills for daily living required by his clients. His goal for growth modifies his previous learning objective, to "know more" about this approach, thus revising his supervisory contract. Administrative goals for growth may call for a change or revision of the contract as well. For example, in the case of Chantey and Billy, a specific goal for growth was negotiated having to do with his lateness (this was a goal for growth that had both clinical and administrative implications).

Administrative responsibilities may change and also require a change in the supervisory contract that has nothing to do with remediation. For example, a staff member may get a promotion or take a new position that has different responsibilities, or a hospital may change methods of record keeping in order to get Medicaid reimbursements that require new methods of documentation, and so on.

Depending on the needs of the client, the supervisee, the agency, professional and legal standards, and the supervisor, supervisees have varying opportunities to create or co-create their goals for growth, action plans, criteria for success, learning objectives, and clinical and administrative responsibilities. In addition, different settings and circumstances may require more or less formal contracts. They may range from verbal and "loose," to written and detailed. Regardless of these specific circumstances, supervisors and supervisees are wise to do some version of contract negotiation and revision in an ongoing way.

6

ᘜ

Intervention

The Supervisor's Clinical Role

This chapter focuses on intervention as it addresses the supervisor's clinical role as facilitator of professional growth. (Chapter 7 addresses intervention from the perspective of the manager's administrative role.) As discussed in the previous two chapters on the work phase, supervisors collect information about the supervisee's work with clients using direct and indirect methods of assessment and then conceptualize themes organized around problems and strengths to be explored in formative assessments. The supervisory pair collaborate on goals for growth based on these themes, and they add to, modify, or replace learning objectives and responsibilities in a revised supervisory contract. In this section, we discuss intervention possibilities that facilitate change or growth, tying these into assessment, goals for growth, and learning objectives to complete the work phase.

Several of the intervention possibilities we summarize here reflect the two main concerns of the supervisor as a facilitator for the supervisee's professional growth: education and empowerment. Teaching, advising, mentoring, consulting, and acting as a sounding board are discussed as part of education. Strength-based approaches fall mainly under empowerment. We then show that many of the core relationship skills can be understood as interventions in and of themselves, manifesting features of education and empowerment. Finally, we discuss interventions related to cultural competence, using Lum's practice process stages and adapting suggestions for a bicultural approach to intervention from Fong, Boyd, and Browne (1999).

These intervention possibilities, as connected to assessments, learning objectives, and goals for growth in the supervisory contract, offer a number of options supervisors can use to facilitate professional growth toward a goal of self-supervision. When supervisors choose from among them (assuming the never-ending development of the supervisory relationship), they are, in effect, doing clinical supervision and answering the "orienting question" suggested in Chapter 1:

> *Given the nature of our relationship (and the level of trust and safety that develops), and what I know about this supervisee (based on my ongoing assessment), how do I intervene (which interventions should I choose to "facilitate the supervisee's professional growth" and "administratively account for the needs of the agency and staff") in ways that help the supervisee reach the learning objectives and goals for growth we have agreed to (in the supervisory contract) and that ultimately best serve clients?*

Before considering these intervention possibilities in greater depth, we should attend to the question asked most frequently by students and seasoned professionals alike when faced with the challenge of deciding on an intervention possibility: "*Which* intervention should I choose?" Most suggestions usually begin with some version of *"It depends!"* To the disappointment of us all, there is no "one size fits all" intervention, no single intervention that facilitates change and optimal functioning that is right for all occasions, for all concerned. However, supervisors can get some guidance when they make informed choices that *depend* on information formulated from the organizing framework we have been discussing as it relates to those whose needs are being met.

Which intervention should I choose?

- *It depends on the needs of the client served:* Interventions that facilitate the supervisee's professional growth should reflect best practices that are safe, knowledgeable, skilled, ethical, legal, culturally competent, and appropriate to the client's problems and strengths as properly assessed in the clinical contract.

- *It depends on the needs of the supervisee:* Interventions should account for the person's developmental level and current extent of knowledge, skills, professional attitudes and values; cultural competence; ethical awareness; experience; learning style; formative and summative evaluations; goals for growth; roles as clinician or service provider, learner, and staff member; and learning objectives and other agreements made in the supervisory contract.

- *It depends on the needs of the agency:* Intervention possibilities should reflect the agency's mission and the kinds of services its staff are able to deliver; interventions should be suggested with an understanding of an appropriate adherence to agency policies and procedures and a knowledge of risk management that is sensitive to ethics codes, legal statutes, and licensing regulations.

■ *It depends on the needs of the profession and laws of the land:* Intervention possibilities should be chosen that reflect ethics codes and educate supervisees about them in concert with academic and professional certification standards. They should also reflect an understanding of legal principles that affect supervisory practice such as standards of care, duty to warn, protect, and report, and so on.

■ *It also depends on the needs of supervisors:* Interventions should be chosen within the limits of their knowledge, skills, professional attitudes, and values as well as the roles they assume as facilitators of professional growth and as managers.

Consider the case of Father Tom, who is dealing with the limitations he is feeling in his new role as supervisor with his supervisor, Father Jim.

Father Tom, who is just beginning his career as a supervisor in the pastoral care department of a large metropolitan hospital, is wrestling with how difficult it is and how much courage it takes to deal with the complicated challenges of doing both his job, working directly with clients, and his "other" job as supervisor of two inexperienced chaplains. He is debating whether to continue in that role, even though he has recently finished his Clinical Pastoral Education (CPE) supervisor's training, with the support of his supervisor/mentor, Father Jim.

He has been concerned, in part, that he is using the precious resources of the department by asking for supervision for himself. Using Father Jim as a sounding board, Father Tom weighs the pros and cons of this decision and he eventually solves his own problem by deciding to stay in the position. Father Jim reminds him that it is not unusual for supervisors, particularly new supervisors, to receive supervision themselves. He provides assurances that Father Tom will receive backup consultation and supervision for his work on a regular basis and coaches him on ways that he could reach his ultimate professional goal: to be the manager of a pastoral care department in a small community hospital.

This information, these assurances, and Father Jim's consultation helps Father Tom solve his problem and supports his decision. Father Jim offers a final piece of advice: "Take good supervision (he always pronounces it with the accent on the first syllable, "super") wherever and whenever it is offered. Add seminars, training conferences, courses, and whatever support you can get; this *is* hard work and you cannot be expected to know what you don't know until you learn it. And to learn it all? That will take more than one lifetime—well after you become the manager of pastoral care at the hospital in small town, USA."

Doing supervision can be a daunting challenge, and it is a lifelong learning experience. Supervisors should take the opportunity to get supervision and continued education throughout their careers and must also give themselves permission to work within their limits as they come to know them over time. We now consider a variety of intervention possibilities available for the supervisor—that should help make the job a bit easier!

EDUCATION

Our consideration of education as a primary intervention in supervision is built on a foundation that assumes the core adult learning principles (Knowles, Holton, and Swanson, 1998) discussed in Chapter 4. As you remember, these principles suggest that adult learners need to understand the value of something before undertaking it; appreciate being seen as capable of self-direction; learn best when tapping into their experience and readiness developmentally; respond to respect for their intrinsic motivation; and have learning orientations that are more amenable to certain approaches than others.

Kadushin's work over the years has been an anchor to discussions related to education and clinical supervision across the helping professions. Kadushin and Harkness (2002, pp. 129–216) review in great depth how "educational supervision" (they says it's another term for "clinical supervision") involves teaching knowledge, skills, and attitudes. They say that

> studies of functions that supervisors identified as those they performed included such educational activities as teaching, facilitating learning, training, sharing experience and knowledge, informing, clarifying, guiding, helping workers find solutions, enhancing professional growth, advising, suggesting, and helping workers solve problems. (p. 129)

The features of educational intervention listed by Kadushin and Harkness can be augmented by several other educationally oriented interventions that we tie to the supervisor's clinical role in Chapter 1 (see Haynes, Corey, and Moulton, 2003, pp. 21–28). In addition to teaching and advising we add mentoring, acting as a sounding board, and consulting. Each provides a different perspective within an educational rubric that can help facilitate professional growth in the work phase toward a goal of self-supervision.

Consider the case of Father Jim and Father Tom as it illustrates several features of an educational intervention. Notice how Father Jim acts as a sounding board for Father Tom. Haynes et al. (2003) suggest that this service provides a safe context in which to process ideas and get objective feedback, particularly in relation to the work situation. By thinking out loud about the pros and cons of staying in his position, Father Tom learns more about his professional needs and consequently decides to stay. Part of his decision is no doubt based on the belief that he could trust his mentor to provide backup and supervision in the future and that this need is not outside the norms of the profession. Haynes and colleagues refer to the mentor as a trusted guide who helps supervisees, especially inexperienced ones, assess their abilities and provides guidance with respect to their future direction.

From a slightly different angle, we see that Father Jim also provides consultation. Haynes and his co-authors (2003) say that consultation involves the use of problem solving in a *specific situation*. The specific situation in this case is Father Tom's ambivalence about whether to stay or go: "The supervisor consults with the supervisee to resolve a problem or to help the supervisee make a decision. . . . The issues addressed can be clinical or administrative and typically focus on the supervisor helping the supervisee to problem solve a situation" (p. 23). We also discuss "consultation" (see the section on group consultation in Chapter 3) as a process in which a supervisor does not have regular, day to day responsibility but is called on as an expert to help solve specific clinical or administrative situations that are particularly difficult.

Finally, we see that Father Jim is not shy about giving advice to Father Tom or coaching him on his goal of managing a pastoral care department in a small community hospital. As Father Tom's adviser for part of his CPE supervisor's training, Father Jim is accustomed to providing specific and directive feedback and does so easily, with his enthusiastic charge to engage in lifelong learning. (Haynes et al. (2003) suggest that this advice-giving function is generally reserved for crisis-oriented situations that call for more immediate and direct action on the part of the supervisor.)

Mentioned but not shown are Father Jim's interventions as a coach. Coaches teach and model and are increasingly building a subspecialty in the helping professions ("life coaching") and business, a new direction that actually has a very strong empowerment orientation. (Hargrove 2000). We turn next to empowerment-oriented interventions; compared to advice, these provide an altogether different yet complementary perspective. Ways to integrate these two points of view *depend,* of course, on the needs of the client, supervisee, agency, profession, the law, and the supervisor as we shall see in the case of Glen and Bill at the end of this section.

EMPOWERMENT

In the context of intervention in the work phase, empowerment approaches allow supervisees to more fully realize and build on their strengths in order to meet their learning objective and goals for growth in the supervisory contract. Zander and Zander (2000, pp. 25–26) refer to this kind of intervention as "giving an A." They suggest assigning the best possible attribution to people's intentions and behavior "up front." In their book, *The Art of Possibility* (2000), they recall Michelangelo as having said that "inside every block of stone or marble dwells a beautiful statue; one need only remove the excess material to reveal the work of art within." They continue, "When you give an A, you find yourself speaking to people not from a place of measuring how they stack up against your standards, but from a place of respect that gives them room to realize themselves. Your eye is on the statue within the roughness of the uncut stone. This A is not an expectation to live up to, but a possibility to live into" (p. 26).

In many ways, the Zanders' point speaks to the assumptions that underlie empowerment interventions. In this section, we briefly revisit the strength-based approaches that we discussed at length in Chapter 5. In the next section, we describe how the core skills, discussed in Chapter 2 as part of engagement, can be considered interventions in and of themselves in the work phase, utilizing a combination of teaching and empowerment strategies. Education as well as empowerment strategies create opportunities to discover the beautiful statue within.

Strength-Based Interventions

In Chapter 5, we discussed the underpinnings of strength-based supervision and outlined the contributions of a number of clinician/researchers. They share several conceptual assumptions that inform our discussion here. A central assumption is that supervisees come for supervision equipped with strengths—skills and attributes—that can be marshaled to assist the clients with whom they work, regardless of their clinical experience and developmental level. While acknowledging that *all* clinicians and supervisees have limitations and room to grow, there is a particular focus on the proficiency and creativity they bring to their clinical work and the supervisory process; the perspectives or co-vision of both the supervisor and supervisee are prized.

There is also a future orientation to the supervision that focuses on consistent collaboration in the creation of learning objectives, goals for growth, action plans, and criteria for success. Supervisor and supervisee take the time to figure out their destinations together as well as the criteria for successful arrival (in essence, the ongoing supervisory contract). Their journey together becomes a matter of using the skills and attributes they both bring to remove obstacles in the road and creatively figure out possibilities and solutions for the best route (in essence, the formative assessment and intervention). *Depending* on the needs of the client, supervisee, agency, profession, the law, and the supervisor, the supervisor is responsible for determining how, when, and if he or she remains in the driver's seat. One of the goals of empowerment—indeed, supervision itself—is to create conditions in which the supervisee goes "solo" and self-supervises (with appropriate consultation when needed, of course).

To remove obstacles and creatively discover possibilities and solutions, supervisors take primary responsibility for designing interventions that seek to amplify the supervisees' existing (but sometimes hidden) expertise in support of their work with clients. Supervisors use scaling questions and internalizing conversations (a "narrative" technique designed to ferret out and focus on internal strengths, described by White & Epston, 1990). They search for exceptions to patterns that may look problematic and build on those. They also ask supervisees to reflect on what works and ask how they got there, going beyond the mutual recognition of a job well done.

If these intervention possibilities sound familiar, congratulations! You have successfully integrated the information in Chapter 5 related to the *formative assessment!* Although each of the strength-based approaches in the literature uses different methods, interventions occur as a function of, or simultaneous to, the process of assessment. Professional growth (the attainment of knowledge, skills, and professional attitudes and values) from the perspective of empowerment is often an outcome based on the *mutual discoveries that take place during assessment.*

Supervisors and supervisees seek, by virtue of these assessment/interventions, to find the "statue within" and the "possibilities they can live into."

CORE RELATIONSHIP SKILLS

There are many features of the core relationship-building skills that can help find the statue within. They can be viewed as interventions in the work phase from both an educational and an empowerment perspective. As mentioned in Chapter 2, the core skills help build trust and safety in the developing supervisory relationship. As interventions in the work phase, they clearly have educative value as they can be used to instruct and facilitate growth as well as model skills supervisees can use with their clients, in the spirit of the dual process. They can also help create opportunities for supervisees to realize and build on strengths as they "live into the possibilities" that meet their learning objectives, goals for growth, and responsibilities in the supervisory contract.

For instance, active listening can help supervisees by providing them room to say what's on their minds. When they hear their own information out loud, they may well hear it in a new way, one that can create a new perspective on an old issue. This is learning that can create new possibilities, particularly when thoughts, feelings, and/or behaviors are validated using a strength-based orientation. (Using active listening in this ways lets supervisors model this skill for supervisees to use with their clients.)

Experiencing the supportive presence and/or the empathy of a supervisor can foster a kind of validation that enhances professional growth (Kadushin and Harkness, 2002). It models and teaches an aspect of relationship development that is important not only in the engagement phase but in the work phase as well. This was illustrated in the case of Donna and Denise who work in the Rehab Center (Chapter 2). Donna's supportive presence over time models a pace that eventually influences Denise's work with patients and staff. It also addresses a basic clinical learning objective in the supervisory contract regarding relationship development.

Self-management skills are skills that supervisees learn in order to deal with feelings, thoughts, and behavior that can adversely affect their professional relationships (e.g., with clients, colleagues, supervisors, managers) if not handled well. In Chapter 2, we highlighted their importance as skills supervisors teach, use, and model as part of building trust and safety in developing supervisory and therapeutic relationships. Now, in the context of intervention, we revisit these methods as supervisors help supervisees learn how to manage their reactions so that they will eventually integrate these methods for themselves as they learn to self-supervise.

In Chapter 2, we described methods supervisors and supervisees use to get in touch with feelings that are outside their awareness. Even when people are in touch with their feelings, these emotions may be so powerful (e.g., anger, anxiety, sadness) that they can interfere with the ability to make thoughtful decisions about a course of action. Supervisors can use, teach, and model several methods to manage strong reactions. Among these are adult time outs and cognitive methods they can use to talk to themselves differently and restructure their thinking (Ellis 1962; Goldfried and Davison, 1976; Meichenbaum and Cameron 1974).

Supervisors are commonly required to help supervisees manage their feelings in situations when reactions to a client may not specifically have to do with that client but are transferred from feelings related to other significant relationships in their lives—so-called countertransference reactions. Supervisors intervene to help their supervisees get in touch with these feelings so they can determine a proper course of action to deal with them. Consistent with the role of facilitating professional growth, supervisors engage in this process so that supervisees eventually internalize these approaches and utilize self-management skills to manage these feelings on their own or appropriately seek consultation. Consider the case example of Drew and his supervisee Brady.

Drew is reviewing videotape of a session that Brady made with his teenage African American client. Brady is a white, middle-aged, relatively new clinician. Drew observes that Brady appeared irritable and impatient with the client throughout the session, an unusual behavior for this normally easygoing psychologist. He asks him questions designed to ferret out what he was feeling, what the difficulty was; he initially focuses on their age and cultural differences.

After processing this information with Drew, who uses many of the core skills we have been discussing, Brady displays a knowing look of understanding and relief. It comes right after Drew tentatively wonders out loud whether these feelings have anything to do with relationships other than the relationship with the client. Brady realizes that his impatience was actually due to the client's pace in making changes related to a weight problem. Brady gets in touch with his fears and anxiety regarding his *son's* struggle in managing his weight. As it turns out, Brady brought a fair amount of emotional baggage with him into the session; this had little to do with the client and a lot to do with a countertransference reaction related to his son. Drew asks Brady if he ever got help dealing with these feelings and his issues with his son. Brady mentions that he will call up his old therapist in order "to do a little work on that."

Drew uses a variety of core relationship skills to help Brady process and discover the basis for his impatient and irritable behavior. When he wonders aloud whether Brady's feelings could have anything to do with other outside relationships, Drew is using a "caring confrontation" skill. Supervisors help supervisees internalize these skills so they can learn to manage their countertransference reactions on their own as part of the goal to self-supervise (or realize that they need help sorting out what they recognize to be a countertransference reaction).

Notice also that Drew *asked* whether Brady had ever gotten help dealing with his feelings about his son; he did not begin to counsel him. This maintains the boundary of working through feelings with an *intent* to facilitate professional growth as opposed to personal growth. It is hoped, of course, that Brady *will grow personally* from this experience as well, but as Kadushin and Harkness (2002, p. 200) suggest, it should be an "unplanned, unintended by-product of the focus on professional growth." We focus next on challenging skills, which form a subset of direct feedback in the intervention phase of supervision.

Challenging skills or caring confrontations are often associated with intervention in the work phase and are a subset of direct feedback methods that teach knowledge, skills, and attitudes in specific instances. Often associated with inappropriate or ineffective behavior, successful challenges or caring confrontations provide feedback that will leave room for the supervisee's observation on identified problems. We see this spirit of collaboration in the case of Marilyn and Jose (Chapter 2) for example, and Drew and Brady earlier in this chapter.

Validation of strengths is another feature of direct feedback that focuses on what works. Supervisees receive direct feedback about successful work and are asked to think about and build on what they already know and do to achieve success. When problematic behavior is observed in the work phase, strength-based feedback seeks to co-create ways to remove obstacles to success in order to meet learning objectives and goals for growth.

The following box shows a set of direct feedback guidelines patterned after Kadushin and Harkness (2002, pp. 160–161) and complemented with several strength-based features.

Guidelines for Successful Direct Feedback

1. Give feedback as soon as possible or at a regularly scheduled supervision session.
2. Be descriptive: Describe how specific behavior "comes across" (focus on behavior, not the person) and how it may be experienced in a less than effective way (if the behavior appears ineffective in relation to its desired objective).
3. Use caring confrontation when feedback focuses on behavior that demonstrates a discrepancy in actions and words and/or feelings. Caring confrontation may also entail challenging ineffective clinical or professional behavior. Egan (2002) reminds us how important it is to be "tactful and tentative in challenging without being insipid or apologetic" (p. 244).
4. Focus on effective behavior as well as ineffective aspects of behavior, and help supervisees consider how they have achieved success. Tie these understandings to ongoing themes that relate to problems and strengths as evaluated in the formative assessment. This method is one of the cornerstones for strength-based interventions.
5. Review how behavior choices are made and discuss and describe possible choice points for increased effectiveness as a way that removes obstacles to success in the future. This is done in a spirit of collaboration or co-creation and therefore reduces the likelihood of defensiveness. This method is another cornerstone for strength-based interventions.
6. Time and timing is important. All learners incorporate information at different rates (as well as in different ways). Supervisors do best when they expect that feedback will be integrated when the supervisee is ready. Remember: Supervision is a process that depends on the needs of clients, supervisees, the agency, profession, the laws, and the supervisor!

Consider next the case of Bill and Glen, which illustrates many of the intervention features discussed earlier and the organizing framework for supervision in general.

Glen was a "star" in his graduate counseling program and was quickly hired to work in the emergency room at the General Hospital following graduation. His supervisor, Bill, was his supervisor for a counseling practicum that he had done in the previous year and had recommended him for the position based partly on that experience. They were both happy to be reunited on the same team, and building on the strength of their previous relationship, there was an easy flow between the two of them for the first few months of the year.

After a while, Bill noticed that Glen was beginning to miss some scheduled family meetings, had failed to write notes in some patients' charts, and said nothing to one of the doctors who rudely and inappropriately chewed him out in front of a patient. Bill questioned his own enthusiasm for Glen and began to hypothesize why he had previously missed these now obvious problems.

Was the day-to-day intensity of working with sick patients and stressed medical staff getting to Glen? Was he reaching his limits of competence and just not suited for this kind of work? Was there something going on in Glen's private life that was getting in the way of his work ethic? Or was this behavior characteristic of a kind of avoiding style?

Bill knew he had to discuss his observations with Glen. Getting in touch with his *own reluctance* to do so mitigated his annoyance at Glen's lack of assertiveness and failure to complete certain tasks. Bill, a 10-year veteran, also considered how stressful the job could be, how difficult it could be to confront the pain of their patients as well as the impatience of a frazzled and frequently overwhelmed medical staff. Bill knew that any confrontation with Glen would be most effective—a true caring confrontation—if he could put himself in a more empathic frame of mind in the spirit of ethical caring. Bill's first step toward intervention was intervening with himself—a kind of self-management in a context of self-supervision.

Bill also realized that Glen was still a bit of a rookie and needed consistent feedback and supervision. He immediately set up a regular supervision schedule: Doing periodic formative assessments would provide both of them a chance to track problems and strengths as well as formulate goals for growth and clarify what would constitute success. When it was time for the hospital's summative evaluation there would be no surprises.

Bill used the next few meetings with Glen to review learning objectives and clinical and administrative responsibilities in the supervisory contract. Because they hadn't had any specific discussions about problems and strengths, it was a good time for Bill to ask Glen about his own observations regarding his performance. He hoped to learn more about Glen's evaluation of himself using verbal report as an indirect method of assessment. His plan was to tie some of the direct observations he made in his own assessment to Glen's and set some new goals for growth based on their co-created findings—a typical strength-based intervention.

Both Bill and Glen had many good things to say about Glen's effectiveness and they spent some time conceptualizing how Glen made these successful interventions. Bill highlighted Glen's expertise using strength-based questions designed to help him reflect further on what was working (e.g., "What told you it was important to get back to the nurse immediately in the Jone's case?"). Initial focus on competence, consistent with an empowerment, education-orientation, provided a supportive atmosphere that set the scene for discussion about the areas requiring further growth.

Bill used Glen's comment, "I feel so uncomfortable meeting with family members at times," as a springboard to discuss Bill's direct observation that Glen was meeting with family members less and less. Part of this supervisor's skill was to discuss a specific behavior in the form of an observation without prejudging its meaning (the basis of a good caring confrontation). Bill used patience in waiting for this theme to present itself as part of Glen's self-evaluation. He could have raised this issue himself, of course, and eventually would have, but by waiting for Glen to mention it, he gained an opportunity to assess for avoidance, an earlier hypothesis.

As the supervisory pair explored the basis for Glen's stated difficulty with families, Bill listened closely to his ideas about the problem. As he listened, it became apparent to Bill that Glen was putting an inordinate amount of pressure on himself to fix the myriad of problems families presented in this crisis environment. As Glen became more and more discouraged and burned out, he began to avoid family meetings. Bill shared this conceptualization as a logical if not positive explanation that fit the facts and feelings ("systemic" family therapists would call this positive or logical connotation). Glen concurred.

Both agreed that avoiding these families would not be an effective choice. Bill might then have chosen to spend more time tapping in to Glen's ideas regarding the different choices he could try. This would have been utilizing more of a strength-based approach. Instead, Bill advised Glen to lower his expectations of what was possible in this setting and learn some new family intervention skills more appropriate to work in the emergency room (like learning to just "be" with family members experiencing a medical emergency). Supervisors have many choice points too; Bill chose to make a specific suggestion, and his advice constituted an education-oriented intervention in this instance that was consistent with Glen's level of development.

Having conceptualized several of these problem themes and having begun to intervene, Glen agreed with Bill to incorporate these new family intervention skills and a change in expectation level as goals for growth that they would monitor together in the context of the supervisory contract. Because Glen offered and Bill agreed that Glen seemed to learn information well using an active experimentation style (an "AE" learning ability—Kolb, 1984) they decided to engage in some role playing (behavior rehearsal) as part of his action plan and as a way to integrate the feedback. They also agreed to monitor Glen's expectations with respect to family interventions in the course of their discussions around case material.

Discussion about Glen's concerns with these families easily connected to his avoidance around charting. Upon close review, it became clear that the charts he avoided were connected to the families he had been avoiding. Bill agreed to coach Glen on additional ways to chart information that would reflect the new family intervention methods he would be using. Evaluating his charts would be used as one way to measure success.

When Bill and Glen came to reviewing Glen's effectiveness with other staff, Bill was tempted to immediately focus on Glen's run-in with "Dr. Rude." He did not fall into the trap, however. It would have been easy to begin thinking about and labeling Glen as an "avoider," a characteristic attribution that might have a grain of truth in it but would leave little room to facilitate change. Instead, Bill stayed focused on Glen's strengths and the specific behaviors they could identify that seemed problematic. Open to hearing Glen's self-evaluation, Bill came to see how actively thoughtful Glen was about his relationships with coworkers. As was the case with his family work, there was no avoidance here either!

As angry as he was with Dr. Rude, Glen admitted that he just *didn't know* the best way to talk with him and preserve their generally good relationship. So, he just did nothing. Bill and Glen discussed and practiced a variety of behavioral choices he could try in similar situations in the future as part of his action plan. (Bill had challenged him to hypothesize what those choices might be, based on his experience with confrontations in other circumstances—a common strength-based intervention.) They agreed to monitor growth in this area in addition to the ones mentioned above, an additional goal for growth in the supervisory contract.

An advantage of their regular supervision meetings was that they would track these problem themes (as well as his strengths), look closely for improvement, and work on removing obstacles in the way of growth over time. An advantage Glen had in this increasingly effective supervisory relationship was that he had a supervisor who would not prematurely turn his hypotheses into assumptions.

In the case of Bill and Glen, Bill intervened with respect to several problem themes in Glen's work with families and other staff. These interventions followed a review of Glen's problems and strengths. Bill collected assessment information from written records, observed Glen's behavior directly, and further reviewed his work indirectly through Glen's self-report. We described several ways Bill used his assessment to first hypothesize and then conceptualize his observations in the formative assessment, co-create goals for growth, and begin to effect action plans and intervene using a combination of education and strength-based methods. His interventions were supportive yet challenging, and they took into consideration Glen's experience and developmental level with respect for his learning style as an adult learner.

Focusing more specifically on Bill's interventions, notice that he first used some self-management skills in relation to his irritation with Glen. He "intervened with himself" (even before meeting with Glen), by restructuring his thinking about Glen's "follow through" problems. He did this by asking himself what I refer to as the "great unhooking question." The question in this case would be something like this: "Why did Glen *need* to avoid certain situations with families and staff?" By framing this question in terms of the necessity of Glen's *available choices*—given what he knows or has learned up to this point— the supervisor is unhooked from assuming the worst.

To the contrary, by framing the question in this way, the supervisor leaves emotional room for Glen's perspective as well as thinking about Glen as doing the best he *currently* knows how to do. (This amounts to giving him the Zanders' "A" up front.) Consequently, both the supervisor and supervisee are freed up to concentrate on future possibilities for growth in an empathic and supportive atmosphere that actually raises the likelihood for growth. This is a good example of a strength-based, education-oriented intervention that relies on the use of the core skills.

Having intervened with himself, Bill was ready to chisel away in search of Glen's statue within—*with* Glen. Remember that Bill invited Glen to consider his own work toward the beginning of their review session. As Glen revealed the areas in which he himself had concern, Bill deftly piggybacked his own observations onto Glen's and used these as the focus for the several interventions he utilized. Glen had been encouraged by Bill to freely share his observations and self-evaluations in an "error acceptance learning" environment (Munson 2002, pp. 241–242).

Bill's interventions were also built on a foundation of good relationship skills and strength-based co-vision that also had an educational quality. He suggested that Glen change his expectations about successful outcome with families in the hospital. He shared knowledge about skills Glen could use with respect to "being with" families in distress. In discussing Dr. Rude, he drew on Glen's previous confrontation experiences and helped him work on choices that could be generalized and transferred to the organizational hierarchy in the hospital—a typical strength-based intervention. He coached and taught Glen ways to chart a great deal of complex information about the family system in a simple and informative way.

The interventions Bill made were done in a way that respected and empowered Glen's opinions and observations; he was open to the possibilities Glen could live into. At the same time, he shared his own perspectives without hesitation and stayed within a hierarchy tempered by the structure and processes of a mutually agreed-on contract for learning and service. This is true education/empowerment orientation to facilitate professional growth. The last of the interventions we examine here relate to Fong, Boyd, and Brown's (1999) suggestions for a biculturalization of interventions model.

CULTURALLY COMPETENT INTERVENTIONS

Beginning with engagement, we have discussed cultural competence with multicultural clients, focusing on ways to help build trust and safety in the supervisory relationship. We highlighted Lum's (2000) practice process stages in engagement and carried it through the work phase, utilizing his model to learn about ways to assess problems and strengths in culturally competent ways. In this chapter, we complete our discussion, keying in on Lum's intervention stage. We follow with an adaptation of the biculturalization of interventions model developed by Fong, Boyd, and Browne (1999).

Lum's Process Stage Approach: Intervention

Lum (2000) suggests that principles of intervention must be developed for each client that are compatible with their ethnosystems. Worker-client (and in our case supervisor–supervisee) tasks involve formulating imaginative interventions that focus on the unique problems of clients in their situations. Lum asserts that each client presents problems that require creative action. He ties creativity and change into a goal orientation similar to the one suggested in our framework, where "goals are terminal, or ultimate, outcomes that the client and worker would like to have achieved upon completion of the intervention phase" (p. 138).

Interventions are task centered and behaviorally oriented for the client and include attention to "large system" change that focuses on "unjust and exploitive social policies, regulatory laws, and institutional practices. Thus, in multicultural practice, intervention must encompass both clinical and community dimensions" (p. 139). Lum specifies a range of methods that informs this outline further, and interested readers are referred to his chapter on intervention principles.

Fong (2001) proposes interventions that are consistent with Lum's call for creative, individualized interventions and suggests that they should be designed and planned on the basis of the "assessed strengths of the client's cultural values" (p. 6). She adds, "To be culturally competent is to know the cultural values of the client system and to use them in planning and implementing services" (p. 6). We consider her biculturalization of interventions model next.

Biculturalization of Interventions Model

Fong (2001, p. 6) cites Fong, Boyd, and Browne, who recommend a biculturalization of interventions model for assessment and intervention when working with multicultural clients. This process involves identifying and selecting
interventions that utilize indigenous approaches, which are compatible and
may be integrated with Western interventions—a model in concert with Lum's
call for "indigenous principles of intervention." The following four steps are an
adaptation of this model that can help supervisors with their supervisees and
supervisees with their clients.

1. Identify cultural values: Supervisors identify values important in the
    supervisee's culture and help supervisees identify values important in the
    client's culture. These can be used to reinforce supervisory and therapeutic
    interventions.

2. Choose and apply compatible Western interventions: Supervisors find and
    use Western interventions that are *compatible* with indigenous interventions
    and support the supervisee's cultural value system. In the same way, the
    supervisor helps the supervisee finds suitable Western interventions
    compatible with indigenous interventions and the client's cultural value
    system.

3. Utilize indigenous interventions: Supervisors analyze and use indigenous
    interventions appropriate to the multicultural differences of the supervisee
    and help supervisees do likewise with their clients.

4. Develop integrated frameworks and approaches: Supervisors and
    supervisees develop frameworks and approaches that can be integrated
    with Western interventions that are compatible with the supervisee's and
    client's cultures.

Consider the case of Aris and Julia, whose couple therapist, Betsy, sought
supervision around a difficult set of circumstances that they were experiencing. The supervisor's suggestions for intervention are based on a biculturalization of interventions.

⚬⚬⚬⚬⚬⚬⚬

Aris and Julia were a middle-aged married couple, who had emigrated
from Cape Verde to the United State in the early 1960s. They made an
appointment for couple therapy at the suggestion of their oldest daughter,
who had just finished her counseling degree and who, coincidentally,
had just moved out of the family home—the last of three children
to do so.

Julia was beside herself with Aris because he wouldn't agree to support her wish to begin college. She argued that her responsibilities as a
homemaker were reduced because the children were no longer living
at home, and she believed she would easily be able to attend college and
still continue her home dressmaking business. While she was adamant

about going to school, she was equally adamant about having Aris's active support and to use her words, "his blessing." They were a married couple and as such, her values demanded that he be in agreement with such an important decision.

Aris felt extremely conflicted. He dearly loved his wife and wanted to remain "happily married" to her; although extremely proud of her intelligence and competence, he was privately worried about what his friends would think if he "let" her go to college. None of the wives of his contemporaries had attended college and he openly confessed that he was more concerned about their reactions than about Julia's actual wish to attend. He felt that he had a certain status to keep as president of his men's social club, and being in that position added to his conflict.

Betsy, who learned this information from Aris in an individual session (a standard part of the initial assessment), experienced no conflict in her opinion about Julia's aspiration. She wholeheartedly supported it! Her conflict, and the reason for the consultation, lay in respecting the couple's values about marriage and Aris's struggles with his peers on one hand, and her strong egalitarian views as both a therapist and a woman on the other hand.

Seeking consultation with Fernanda, an older Portuguese family therapist familiar with Cape Verdian culture, Betsy was challenged to create an intervention for the couple that was compatible with their values and that solved their dilemma, without compromising her own beliefs and values. Fernanda was called on to share her experience and knowledge and help this marriage counselor find an appropriate intervention. Following a detailed assessment of the situation, Fernanda made some specific suggestions that both agreed might fit the bill.

First, Betsy empathized with Aris in a private session about how difficult it must be for him to have one foot in the traditional culture of his social club and the other foot in the Western U.S. culture, a culture in which many American middle-aged, "stay at home" wives who were essentially finished with child care and wanted to start college, frequently received family support.

Then, knowing that Aris was proud of his wife and her accomplishments, basically in agreement with her wish to attend school, and feeling quite miserable about the current state of affairs, Betsy made a specific suggestion that worked. She confirmed with him that as president of his social club, he had surely garnered the respect of his peers as a leader. He agreed. She then wondered aloud with him about how the members would react if he, as a forward looking leader, *proudly encouraged* his wife's wish to be in school. That she would continue her home business at the same time was also surely consistent with their values of hard work and achievement. He said he would think about it.

When Betsy next greeted the couple for what turned out to be their last session, she knew something had changed. Sitting next to each other on the therapy couch, Julia shared her delight about how they were now in agreement about college and that she had already enrolled in her first class! She was practically beaming when she also acknowledged (with a slight wink) that somehow Aris was even beginning to talk about the decision as if it was his idea in the first place.

Although there was a part of Betsy that cringed when she heard that last statement, there was also a part of her that celebrated an outcome that was successful for her clients. This was an outcome whose likelihood for success was increased because of her determination to remain consistent with the values and culture of her clients. She did this in a way that successfully utilized a biculturalization process (Fong, 2001) and did not compromise her integrity as a therapist.

7

🌿

Intervention

The Supervisor's Administrative Role

This chapter focuses on intervention as it addresses the supervisor's administrative role as manager. When we discussed the roles of the supervisor in Chapter 1, we noted that supervisors who work in agency settings fulfill some administrative functions that relate to their clinical work even if they are not formally designated managers. Managers, as well as everyone else working in an agency setting, function foremost to carry out the mission of the agency in service to the welfare of its clients. Clinical supervisors have several other functions that relate to their managerial role, which we discuss in this chapter. These are considered interventions that complete the work phase vis-á-vis administrative responsibilities. These interventions primarily account for the needs of the agency (which in most cases simultaneously attends to requirements of the profession and the laws of the land) and the needs of the staff as they relate to the agency setting.

We focus on two general intervention areas: ensuring proper risk management (including special attention to legal and ethical issues and the summative evaluation) and negotiating a fit between the needs of the agency and the needs of the supervisee as staff member. In this last section we discuss a "win-win" negotiating strategy that managers can use to facilitate that fit. We begin our discussion with interventions that ensure proper risk management.

RISK MANAGEMENT

Ensuring that staff follow risk management policies is usually discussed as an intervention in relation to the agency's needs as well as an intervention designed to protect the interests of the client. In fact, such interventions also protect the supervisee and the supervisor, both of whom work according to the ethical standards of their professions and under the laws of the land.

Supervisors' Actions that Minimize Liability Risks

Haynes, Corey, and Moulton (2003, pp. 192-206) provide an excellent overview of risk management that features 14 possible actions supervisors can take to minimize liability risks. Below is an outline that lists the actions they describe, reprinted from their book (p. 194). We reviewed most of these risk management strategies in our discussion of the supervisory contract and the ethical use of self in Chapter 2.

- Don't supervise beyond your competence
- Evaluate and monitor supervisee's competence
- Be available for supervision consistently
- Formulate a sound supervision contract
- Maintain written policies
- Document all supervisory activities
- Consult with appropriate professionals
- *Maintain working knowledge of ethics codes, legal statutes, and licensing regulations*
- Use multiple methods of supervision
- *Practice a feedback and evaluation plan*
- Purchase and verify professional liability insurance coverage
- Evaluate and screen all clients under supervisee's care
- Establish a policy for ensuring confidentiality
- Incorporate informed consent in practice

Legal Statutes and Ethical Implications

As mentioned in Chapter 2, codes of ethics and ethical norms sometimes serve as benchmarks for legally evaluating professional behavior (Levy 1993). Take for example the notion of the "standard of care." Falvey (2002, p. 15) writes that the standard of care is an expectation "that our professional activities must be consistent with what similarly trained professionals would do under similar circumstances." This standard is often used to interpret legal statutes, and supervisors are responsible to keep up with their constant evolution not only to ensure proper risk management on behalf of the agency, their supervisees, and themselves, but also to provide ethical service. Following is a glossary of legal principles reprinted from Haynes et al. (2003, p. 184). We take a closer look at the duties to warn, protect, and report in the context of the limits of confidentiality following this outline.

Legal Principles that Affect Supervisory Practice

- *Standard of Care:* The normative or expected practice performed in a given situation by a given group of professionals
- *Statutory Liability:* Specific written standard with penalties imposed, written directly into the law
- *Negligence:* When one fails to observe the proper standard of care
- *Negligent Liability:* When one fails to provide an established standard of care
- *Vicarious Liability:* Being responsible for the actions of others based on a position of authority and control
- *Direct Liability:* Being responsible for your own actions of authority and control over others
- *Privileged Communication:* The privilege allowed an individual to have confidential communications with a professional. It prevents the courts from requiring revelation of confidential communication
- *Duty to Warn:* The obligation of a therapist whose client presents a serious danger of violence to another person to warn and protect the third party
- *Duty to Protect:* The obligation of a therapist to take the necessary steps to protect a client with suicidal intent
- *Duty to Report:* The obligation of a therapist to report abuse or suspected abuse of children or the elderly in a timely manner

Limits of Confidentiality and the Duties to Warn, Protect, and Report

Supervisors need to be knowledgeable not only about the importance of confidentiality, but also the limits of what can be kept confidential. This information applies to supervisees in relation to their clients and supervisors in relation to their supervisees. (Should there be problems assessed in the work phase with respect to supervisees and clients, supervisors work with their supervisees to set up the appropriate goals for growth, action plans, and criteria for success.)

Falvey (2002) suggests that supervisees inform their clients of confidentiality limits in informed consent procedures (preferably in writing and orally), noting that Swenson calls this a "clinical Miranda warning." She also advises that supervisors use informed consent procedures with their supervisees in matters that relate to confidentiality. In their gatekeeping role, supervisors are often called on to release information to academic institutions, licensing boards, future employers in the form of references, and the agency itself (in terms of evaluations). Typical limitations to confidentiality that relate to clients include authorized billing to third party payers and fee collection services and situations mandated by the courts. In addition, Falvey cautions, both supervisors and supervisees have "the duty to warn" potential victims of dangerous clients, the "duty to protect" clients at risk of serious harm to themselves, and the "duty to report" certain information revealed in confidence. It is important to know the implications of these last three mandates.

The "duty to warn" is probably best known by virtue of the *Tarasoff v. Regents of the University of California* (1976) case in which the treating psychologist and supervising psychiatrist were found liable for failure to warn the intended victims of violent clients. Falvey (2002) provides an excellent overview of this case and the current legal and ethical status of this mandate. She reports that while only 14 jurisdictions have adopted this ruling specifically into law, it is in essence becoming a national standard of care (p. 95).

Although it is difficult for anyone to absolutely predict intended violence, Falvey reviews the following predictors: "Past violent behaviors, specific or detailed threats, threats repeated on numerous occasions, violent ideation and poor impulse control, expressed fear of the client by others, possession of the means to carry out a threat, a history of irrational or unpredictable behavior, and the existence of a likely precipitant" (p. 97). There are also no absolute guidelines that determine who to warn, but reviewing *Tarasoff*, Falvey (2002) suggests at minimum that the police should be notified as well as the intended victim and those who might be able protect the victim. In addition, she cautions that supervisors are expected to monitor and help meet these requirements.

Supervisees must also break confidentiality with a "duty to protect" when clients threaten serious self-injury such as suicide. Falvey suggests that supervisors monitor these threats and arrange for adequate training for their supervisees, as well as consider directly intervening themselves to assess for lethality when supervisees are unlicensed and/or undertrained. Falvey also reports that there is debate in the courts and in the field about who is responsible for suicide, but there is general consensus that if predicted, professionals are required to act to prevent it. She suggests that affirmative actions, such as contacting police, family, and emergency services, are predicated on the basis of "clear," "immediate," "serious," and/or "imminent" danger.

Falvey (2002, p. 100) asserts that the supervisee (and supervisor by extension) may be held liable if there is assistance (e.g., paradoxical suggestion), negligent diagnosis, or abandonment. "Abandonment" occurs when the clinician inappropriately ends treatment, such as ending a counseling relationship without notice or planned termination. Most ethics codes make reference to abandonment, which has become a particularly important principle as it relates to managed care. Haynes et al. (2003) cautions that there may be an ethical dilemma for the clinician (and by extension, the supervisor) if termination is decided by the managed care provider instead of being a collaborative process between counselor and client.

Because laws vary by jurisdiction and codes are different across states and professions, Falvey (2002) suggests that supervisors and supervisees would do well to stay informed about recent developments in suicide prevention and the duty to protect. Finally, supervisors and supervisees should freely consult with colleagues and other trained professionals as well as document all steps taken as a demonstration of sound judgment. (We review several of these steps in the next section on ethical decision making.)

A third major limit to confidentiality lies in the "duty to report," which is mandated in some states and/or ethics codes to protect the elderly and/or persons who are considered vulnerable due to mental or physical disabilities. Practitioners across all helping professions and legal jurisdictions are mandated to report child abuse and neglect under the Child Abuse Prevention and Treatment Act of 1974 (PL 93-247). Falvey (2002) reports that mental health professionals are granted immunity for breaking confidentiality when acting in good faith and that states often hold mandated reporters liable if they fail to report.

These guidelines seem more straightforward than is the case in practice, and states vary in terms of how they interpret certainty of abuse, origin of information, and timing of the actual report. In addition, many practitioners admit failing to report because of "concern for child safety, cultural differences in child rearing, fear of alienating clients, confidentiality rights, age of the child, type of abuse, and lack of familiarity with or confidence in the child protective services to whom reports are made" (Falvey 2002, p. 101).

Supervisors have the responsibility to ensure that their supervisees understand and adhere to the ethics codes under which they practice as well as fulfill their responsibilities to act within the laws of the land. When the two conflict, supervisors and supervisees alike are left to wrestle with dilemmas between legal obligations like the duty to report (as well as warn and protect) and ethics codes that speak to the rights of confidentiality and self-determination.

What is a supervisor to do? Ethical decision making is a method supervisors can use and teach their supervisees to use in situations involving an ethical dilemma.

Ethical Decision Making

An ethical dilemma involves making a choice between equally unsatisfactory alternatives of a difficult problem that seems to have no acceptable solution. Reamer (1995, p. 4) refers to this as a "situation where professional duties and obligations, rooted in core values, clash. These are the instances when workers must decide which values—as expressed in various duties and obligations—will take precedence."

Given the likelihood that supervisees will face these kinds of conflicts and dilemmas when called on to intervene, it is important for supervisors to teach a way to think about and resolve these difficulties. Reamer (1995, pp. 64–65) has provided a process for ethical decision making:

1. Identify the ethical issues, including the values and duties that conflict.

2. Identify the individuals, groups and organizations who are likely to be affected by the ethical decision.

3. Tentatively identify all possible courses of action and the participants involved in each, along with the possible benefits and risks for each.

4. Thoroughly examine the reasons in favor of and opposed to each possible course of action, considering relevant:

   ■ Ethical theories, principles and guidelines;

   ■ Codes of ethics and legal principles;

   ■ Practice theory and principle;

   ■ Personal values (including religious, cultural, and ethnic values and political ideology), particularly those that conflict with one's own.

5. Consult with colleagues and appropriate experts (such as agency staff, supervisors, agency administrators, attorneys, ethics scholars).

6. Make the decision and document the decision-making process.

7. Monitor, evaluate, and document the decision.

This model for ethical decision making is extremely useful, particularly in complicated and involved ethical/legal circumstances. People choosing to work in the helping professions do not generally choose to be lawyers; however, in our increasingly litigious society, supervisors would do well to understand the wide range of legal considerations mentioned above. The informed supervisor (and clinician) will want to read Falvey's (2002) *Managing Clinical Supervision* and Reamer's (2003) *Social Work Malpractice and Liability* as well as pertinent chapters in Bernard and Goodyear (1998) and Haynes, Corey, and Moulton (2003). We turn next to another important feature of risk management, the summative evaluation.

The Summative Evaluation

Most clinical supervisors in managerial roles are responsible to formally evaluate their supervisee/staff members. Agency evaluations are used to monitor the quality of work related to clients as well as to the mission and needs of the organization. Supervisors also use formal evaluations to attest to the competence of supervisees as they perform gatekeeping functions at the request of degree-granting institutions, state licensing boards, and accreditation bodies. We refer to these kinds of evaluations as summative evaluations in contrast to the formative assessments that provide the supervisee with feedback geared mainly to facilitate professional growth.

Whenever professional gatekeeping functions are involved and judgments are requested, there is a strong likelihood for tension if not full-blown anxiety (on the part of both supervisor and supervisee)—especially if the outcome could alter the path of the supervisor's career. Tension and the accompanying threat to trust and safety exist whenever there is a power differential and an evaluative process where *any* unfavorable consequence is even a *possibility*.

Shulman's Seven-step Evaluation Process In this section we summarize a seven-step evaluation process offered by Shulman (1993, pp. 206–208), which is highly sensitive to the delicate nature of the evaluation interactions and is particularly compatible to the organizing framework presented in this book.

We then outline several intervention methods that complement Shulman's framework and that can manage and mitigate possible tension, maintain a supportive atmosphere, and still fulfill the accountability functions of the summative evaluation.

1. Supervisors provide supervisees with a guide to the evaluation process at the beginning of the relationship. The guide spells out areas that will be assessed and what the evidence will be for work completed. This is similar to provisions incorporated in the supervisory contract such as clinical and administrative responsibilities, learning objectives, goals for growth, action plans, and criteria for success. It also fulfills the ethical obligation for informed consent.

2. These items should be referred to periodically and become a natural feature of the supervisory process. This step is incorporated into the very nature of the framework here and is part and parcel of the supervisory process itself.

3. Periods of assessment before the formal evaluation should be built into the process so that supervisor and supervisee can track progress and flag areas that need concentration and also to avoid surprises. A positive aspect of an evaluation guide is that it continually helps in the identification of "the learning agenda." This parallels the direct feedback process and use of the formative assessment, which summarizes themes, organized around problems and strengths and forms the basis of the goals for growth as discussed in this text.

4. Both the supervisor and supervisee take responsibility to review the evaluation guide and prepare a preliminary assessment. This begins a process of collaboration regarding the actual evaluation document. It provides an opportunity to process any hesitation or resistance early on so that the evaluation is ultimately experienced as a joint venture and "not simply as something the supervisor does to the supervisee" (Shulman 1993, p. 207).

5. Both supervisor and supervisee should provide some documentation for their views that details and illustrates strengths and weaknesses. If good documentation is maintained with the evaluation in mind, the writing is much simpler. Supervisors should consider expanding standard evaluation forms if the ones used do not provide enough room for meaningful expression. Tracking strengths and weaknesses is built into the organizing framework here, and documentation is a concrete manifestation of the work done. It not only provides an important reminder of the work, but it also covers ethical and legal responsibilities related to informed consent and due process.

6. A joint meeting is set up to discuss versions of the preliminary evaluation drafted by supervisor and supervisee. The pair should go through each section and comment on areas of agreement and disagreement, allowing enough time to negotiate differences. Supervisors begin the meeting with a brief summary of both strengths and weaknesses and then ask

supervisees what they would like to attend to first. They generally like to begin with the problems and avoid the suspense of waiting until the end; in reality, supervisees have a difficult time hearing the strengths until discussion about limitations is out of the way.

7. Finally, it is up to the supervisor to make decisions about the content of the evaluation. Should the supervisee disagree with the final document (following ample opportunity to negotiate differences), there should be some notation made to that effect in the final form.

No wonder tension is a companion to the evaluation process. This is hard work! But as Shulman (1993) points out, proper attention to these steps pays dividends to the supervisee, supervisor, and "ultimately, the service" (p. 208). Several intervention methods, discussed next, can help manage the inherent tension attendant on the process; they underscore and complement many of suggestions made in Shulman's framework.

Managing Tension Despite high probabilities for success using Shulman's model, evaluation time is still often a difficult time for many supervisors and their supervisees. Several intervention methods, however, are available to supervisors to manage the tension and discomfort of this process and to help manage the needs of the staff as they relate to the agency setting. Managers can utilize a "powering with" style that we first talked about in Chapter 2; work to ensure clarity in roles, responsibilities, and learning objectives, goals for growth, action plans, and criteria for success—provisions essentially included in the ongoing supervisory contract; and diligently provide regular and frequent feedback throughout the supervisory process. We comment on each below.

If supervisors mainly rely on the inherent power they have over their supervisees to manage their work, it can adversely affect their supervisees' self-esteem and professional self-efficacy, which in turn can affect the quality of their service. On the other hand, when supervisors favor a "powering with" style and utilize an attitude of ethical caring, a synergy is created that pools the wisdom and resources of both the supervisor and supervisee. Now possibilities to "live into" are heightened from the perspective of the supervisee and the probabilities for increased productivity are increased from the perspective of the agency. Now the tension is reduced.

Doing evaluations and giving feedback are continuous tasks in supervision, and there are always elements of judgment involved. Skilled feedback, however, need never be judgmental and supervisors who think in terms of caring confrontations, co-vision, error acceptance learning, and "giving an A" truly facilitate the professional growth of the supervisee *and* the needs of the agency.

Feedback about performance that is handled well is built on a foundation of clarity about aspects of the ongoing supervisory contract as outlined above. Expectations are clear, responsibilities are clear, desirable outcomes are clear, action plans are clear, criteria for success are clear. Everyone is on the same train tracking progress together from formative assessments through to the summative evaluation in the context of the ongoing supervisory contract. Being clear and explicit not only reduces potential conflict and tension, but it also paves an unob-structed path to success. (As Yogi Berra might say, if you travel *together* to a clearly defined destination using the same road, you might end up at the same place!)

A variety of prescribed instruments are used by agencies and accrediting bodies to format their summative evaluations. They may use narratives, Likert-type instruments to quantify impressions, behavior checklists, or others (see Bernard Goodyear 1998, pp. 161–163, for an in-depth summary). One method, management by objectives (MBO), supports the importance of clarity as reflected in the supervisory contract. Hersey and Blanchard (1982, pp. 119–120) describe this approach, introduced by Peter Drucker in the organizational management literature. It relates particularly well to the evaluation of admin-istrative (and clinical) responsibilities specified in the supervisory contract. MBO is basically a process whereby the supervisor and supervisee identify common goals and major areas of responsibility in terms of expected results. These measures are used to guide operations of a work unit and evaluate the contributions of each member.

Regardless of the format used, it is important to be diligent and do regular and frequent formative assessments to manage tension and anxiety and to ensure that there are no surprises in the summative evaluation. Supervisors and supervisees often avoid formative assessments because they anticipate the dis-comfort that comes with discussing limitations in the work. "Discomfort leads to resistance, clarifying why the lack of timely feedback has become the most common basis of formal ethics complaints regarding supervision" (Koocher and Keith-Spiegel, cited in Falvey 2002, p. 107)

But doing regular and frequent formative assessments (particularly ones that balance attention to problems and strengths) actually protects against dis-comfort. As supervisees get feedback early (and continuously), anxiety and ten-sion is reduced because they essentially become desensitized to the process, which is seen as a normal part of business (compared to a yearly evaluation, for example). Anxiety is often a function of uncertainty, and getting regular, pre-dictable feedback helps supervisees know where they stand as they participate in determining the goals for growth around problems, action plans, and crite-ria for success. Tension is further reduced when they have a sense that change will be noticed; that they have room to move toward success that will be rec-ognized and time to make the changes required.

When strengths are punctuated as part of a balanced formative assessment, good feelings compete with anticipated discomfort. Giving attention to the supervisee's self-evaluation increases feelings of empowerment, which then compete with anxiety. (Bill did that when he utilized a kind of co-vision by asking Glen about his perceptions and evaluation of his own work.) When coupled with such empowering principles as "giving the A," caring confronta-tion, and error acceptance learning as well as clarity about expectations and criteria for success, feedback in regular formative assessments is not only acceptable to supervisees, it is welcomed.

The responsibilities of clinical supervisor/managers go beyond ensuring that risk management strategies are enforced and summative evaluations completed.

We turn next to discuss the supervisor's role as middle manager and the responsibility to manage the fit between the needs of the agency and the needs of the staff.

MANAGING THE AGENCY-STAFF FIT

Managers are key members of the agency and have a major role in helping to implement the day-to-day operations of the organization. Even if they are not members of upper management and do not have direct policy-making responsibilities (although in many smaller agencies they do), they can have a great impact on how and what services are delivered. This fulfills part of their responsibility to support the mission of the agency on behalf of excellent services for clients. Helping to manage day-to-day operations also includes monitoring the administrative responsibilities of staff and appropriately collaborating with them to construct goals for growth, action plans, and criteria for success when there are problems related to policies and procedures in the work phase of supervision.

In addition, the manager provides the closest link to the welfare of staff. Attending successfully to the needs of staff obviously benefits staff directly, but it also benefits their clients as well as the organization. Clearly, clients benefit from improved service as their clinicians' training needs are addressed and they grow professionally. The organization as a business is benefited because the staff delivers the product! All things being equal, when the product is delivered well, the organization does well. The organization also benefits when staff are well taken care of because retention of good staff is as major a financial consideration for social and health service agencies as it is for any other business.

Supervisors/managers fulfilling these important functions most often act as middle managers. They usually are "in the middle," representing the administrative and psychological needs of the agency on one hand and the administrative and psychological needs of staff members on the other. By the way they manage the responsibilities that come from being in the middle (managers often complain that they're usually in the middle of a lot of trouble!), they can have a powerful impact on how well the organization functions and how clients and staff members are served. We discuss below some of the administrative and psychological needs of the agency and the staff as well as a strategic intervention managers can use to help negotiate the fit between the two.

Administrative and Psychological Needs of the Agency

The administrative needs of the agency basically require managers to interpret, monitor, and implement policies and procedures as they relate to staff. In other words, the organization entrusts them with the task of making sure that staff follow the policies and procedures and carry out the practical responsibilities agreed to in the supervisory contract, sometimes referred to as the work contract. The staff member contracts to carry a certain workload according to the productivity requirements needed to keep the agency afloat, documents interactions related to clients, follows risk management procedures that involve ethics and the law, participates in evaluations, gets proper certifications and licenses, and fulfills other essential duties

Kraines (1991) also posits a psychological contract. As representatives of the organization, managers ask the staff to utilize resources of the agency in good faith and as intended. In addition, management asks that the work be done with a positive attitude and a spirit of cooperation and flexibility, which also supports the work of others and the mission of the agency. This positive attitude is difficult to evaluate formally, but it is often crucial to an atmosphere of cooperation and teamwork in the agency. Using the resources of the agency in good faith can be more easily measured when they are misused. Consider this case example.

Lex had been hired to coordinate and provide in-home respite care services for families who had children with severe disabilities. He supervised three home care specialists and was paid a base salary. He was paid a separate "fee for service" for the visits he made himself. The children loved him. Their parents loved him. His supervisees loved him. The agency loved him. The foundation that sponsored the grant that paid him loved him too. Until they fired him.

Patty, the supervising grant administrator, noticed that Lex couldn't possibly have completed the number of hours and home visits that he had documented, given the number of "active" families on the case list. Families were eligible for only a certain number of visits. When asked about this, Lex averred that this was simply a case of sloppy record keeping. Patty accepted this explanation at first and tracked his hours and record keeping more closely. Upon further review, she realized that Lex had been meeting with families who were no longer on the list of eligible clients and billing the grant for that time. Some might say "he was helping people; let it go." Unfortunately, Lex was simultaneously charging a fee directly to the families he was visiting (they rightfully believed that as former clients of the granting agency they were supposed to pay a fee). The clients were happy to pay his fee. Patty and her grant were not happy to pay it again.

Fortunately, such fraudulent abuses are rare, and managers are more often called on to track use of agency resources that have to do with basic responsibilities related to productivity and risk management. We turn next to the administrative and psychological needs of the staff member.

Administrative and Psychological Needs of the Staff

As representatives of the staff, managers attend to a number of their administrative needs. That helps fulfill the agency's end of the work contract. (Managers spend a great deal of time and energy managing the fit between the organization's perception of productive output and the staff members' perception of what constitutes a job well done and their capacity to do it.) Staff need clear expectations about their job responsibilities and criteria for success, assignments that maximize their abilities, and the time and resources to complete them. In addition, staff require sufficient training to do their jobs well and learning opportunities that facilitate their ideas for professional growth and development. (Obviously, there can be a fair amount of variability from one staff member to the next.)

Consider the following case illustration using an intervention that manages apparently conflicting needs of the agency and the supervisee. This is an example of what is known as win-win negotiating (which we discuss more fully later in this section) and is also a good example of "powering with":

We discussed the case of Tim and Lana in Chapter 5. As you remember, Tim had been interested in learning about cognitive behavioral approaches and revised his contract to include a specific goal for growth "to 'do' effective cognitive behavioral interventions as they relate to the skills for daily living required by his clients." What we don't mention in that case example was Lana's challenge to manage the fit between one of the agency's policies regarding treatment and Tim's idea of what constituted professional growth and development for himself as the two were in conflict. In brief, the community support unit they both worked on used a case management approach to practice and specified teaching clients "skills for everyday living" as a major policy. Anything having to do with therapy was strongly discouraged.

Because of her inherent power as supervisor, Lana had the potential "power over" Tim to nix his learning objective outright. Instead, she chose to "power with" Tim and work with him to frame his goals in a way that satisfied both the policy of the agency and his objectives to learn and use cognitive behavioral (therapeutic) approaches. Lana understood that many elements of cognitive behavior therapy are skill oriented and that they may easily be translated conceptually into skills for everyday living. She agreed to spend supervision time with Tim reviewing how the *concepts* of cognitive behavior therapy offered a way of facilitating skills for everyday living with the clients in the agency. Tim agreed not to refer to his work with clients using the term *therapy* in any of his formal documentation and skillfully framed his goal for growth to include the phrase, "as they relate to the skills for daily living required by his clients."

Lana also agreed to raise the issue of making the organization's policies about treatment protocols more inclusive at her next management meeting. (As mentioned, managers are often in a position to negotiate changes in the system by their position in the agency's hierarchy.) In this case, Lana evidenced a classic win/win negotiation strategy as she worked with Jim in a way that satisfied his needs, the needs of the agency, and the needs of the agency's clients. We discuss this win-win strategy further following discussion of the staff's psychological needs.

In addition to the responsibility of attending to the administrative needs of staff, the manager is challenged to help create a safe, trustworthy, and healthy work atmosphere to help meet the psychological needs of the staff. When managers are successful, some of their own needs to provide nurturing may be met; they also help support conditions that raise the likelihood that staff will enthusiastically and cooperatively commit to the agency and get the job done well.

An important provision of the psychological contract is to provide staff with rationales for agency policies and procedures that affect them and the services they provide to clients. As discussed in Chapter 3, adults "need to know why." They also need a way to channel their observations about rules affecting their work into possibilities for productive change. When Lana said she would raise the issue of expanding treatment protocols at her management meeting, she was attending to Tim's psychological needs. Everyone benefits from this. Staff is a rich source of information about how to best deliver the product. If decision making in the agency is decentralized enough and the hierarchy flexible enough to allow for input from "below," the organization will benefit from the feedback, staff will feel empowered in their workplace, and of course, clients will be the ultimate beneficiaries.

Another psychological need staff have relates to feeling that they are getting paid a salary commensurate with their workload. Productivity demands are usually fairly heavy in social and health service settings, and as Kadushin and Harkness (2002) point out, salaries are often seen as an objective measure of one's worth. The actual dollars a staff member receives is certainly important, but not as important as equity. Kadushin and Harkness say that equity "requires remuneration consistent with one's workload, performance, and reference group peers" (p. 241). Equitable pay also accounts for comparisons among people who are comparably educated and who have similar achievements and background.

Win/Win Negotiation Intervention Strategy

Whether they are negotiating equitable salaries or other psychological and administrative needs of the staff and the agency, middle managers are often in the middle. Some supervisors respond to this difficult position at one end of the continuum by adopting a top-down communication style that focuses on ways to get staff to follow agency directives. They often feel a strong squeeze from below when staff do not like the directives or just react negatively to the manner in which they are related.

Supervisors at the other end of the continuum become champions for the staff and find themselves regularly tangling with upper management; they often feel a squeeze from above. Others find a way out of the middle, as did Lana in the last case, by using a win-win negotiation approach (Fisher and Ury, 1991). There are several steps to this basic strategic intervention: The first step involves searching for an outcome goal that is mutually beneficial and desirable to all parties and that speaks to each side's underlying interests. When the focus is on one's interests, one can avoid getting stuck defending a rigid position. Thus, using the last case example, discussion is not focused so that the outcome is either cognitive behavior therapy *or* skills for daily living. In that case, there would be only two choices, two positions: "my way"—"your way" and discussion can end up with one side arguing to *convince* the other side that they are right.

Instead, thinking or discussion involves a goal that is amenable to both sides and that reflects their underlying interests. In the last example, that would be something like "use interventions that help clients learn skills for daily living (the interests of the agency) and at the same time, help Tim learn and provide interventions using concepts from a cognitive behavioral point of view (Tim's interest)." Sometimes called a mutual benefit statement (Negotiation Training, 2001), this outcome statement satisfies the interests of *both* parties.

The next step is to creatively reach this goal in a way that everyone can live with. The assumption here is that there is a difference between means and ends. Once the ends are in agreement, one searches for the means to satisfy the agreed-on mutual benefit statement and each side's underlying interests. In this case, the means both sides can live with is for Tim to "provide interventions to clients that are *conceptually* oriented to skills for daily living, including interventions from the cognitive behavioral approach." This is the win/win. It includes possibilities for learning and using cognitive behavioral approaches that are focused on skills for daily living. This meets Tim's interests and the interests of the agency and its clients.

Consider the following example of a supervisor who is skilled in thinking "win/win." She was given the directive to "do something about the inconsistent and poor quality of record keeping in your department—now!"

<hr>

Alexis had been hired just one month prior to receiving this charge from her director, and she is still orienting herself to the agency and developing relationships with her staff. Her staff is a very experienced, dedicated but undertrained group of case managers working in a special outpatient program for people who are physically disabled with chronic disease. As she reviews their records, she finds herself agreeing with the assessment of her director (if not the rude manner in which the information had been delivered to her).

Alexis brings up "records" as an agenda item in the regular staff meeting. She begins by asking staff how *they* feel about the state of their record keeping. She knows to ask them about their perspective first so she can assess their needs and wishes regarding this administrative responsibility. The group members are somewhat reticent to speak at first, but following some minimal encouragement for the "truth," they move into a resounding chorus of curses and complaints. She is surprised by how strong their feelings are until she learns that they have been crit-icized for *years* about the quality and inconsistency of their records.

She asks how this could go on for so long. Almost in unison, the group members agree that they do not fully understand how to write their notes for the DAP (Data-Assessment-Plan) system the agency uses, despite several training sessions about how to enter information into the system. When Alexis asks them how they feel about taking notes in the first place, they make it clear that no one likes to do them! At the same time, this veteran staff adds that they realize the clinical necessity of good notes and that their funding and therefore their jobs are dependent on adequate record keeping.

Alexis understands that good, consistent record keeping includes yet goes beyond knowing a system for organizing entries; consistency across staff calls for agreement about a conceptual framework that organizes their thoughts about the work, and good notes become a reflection of clear thinking. She offers these thoughts to her staff and reviews their sentiments about the importance of good, consistent records in the form of an outcome goal or "mutual benefit statement" (a statement that is mutually beneficial to the staff and the charge of the director). She says, "Can we agree then, that a good goal for the team is to develop a more consistent way to think about and write better notes?" There is easy agreement. She asks if they have ideas about how to make that happen (thus finding a means to that end). There is easy agreement about that too. They request training together as a team (they pick up Alexis' use of the term *team* for the first time) so that everyone is in accord as they go forward. Alexis agrees and tells them that she will follow up on *their* request right away and discuss the details at their next staff meeting.

Alexis employs the use of win-win negotiating in a way that satisfies both the needs of the agency and the needs and wishes of her staff. Her first step is to listen and learn where her staff stands on the issue. Next, she frames their understanding about the need for good and accurate record keeping as a goal that they could and obviously do buy into. In doing this, she achieves the single most important step in any negotiation, which is to discover mutually ben-eficial goals (based on underlying interests) that all parties can agree to—at the start. The final step involves discovering acceptable means to achieve the goal, now that there is agreement on the desirable outcome. The team makes the obvious choice—for appropriate training—a choice that Alexis and the agency can deliver on.

Alexis uses the staff meeting time to manage some of the administrative responsibilities included in everyone's supervisory contracts, and she does so by negotiating in a way that keeps her from being squeezed from above and below in the organizational hierarchy. At the same time, she uses this occasion as an opportunity to strengthen her "team" and build a more supportive relationship with them as a group. This clearly meets some of the psychological needs of both the staff and the agency: to function in a healthy and safe working environment in which there are positive attitudes and a spirit of cooperation.

This chapter has reviewed several of the administrative responsibilities most clinical supervisors, like Alexis, are asked to carry out in an agency setting. There are a number of other administrative tasks that many managers assume that relate, for example, to organizational development, personnel policies, fundraising, and so on. These features go beyond the scope of this book and are well covered elsewhere in the literature.

A Final Note

A relatively new supervisor whose work I had just begun to supervise read the final draft of this book and commented that she felt both better and worse for the experience. She felt better because she now has a clearer picture of what supervision is all about, including a better understanding of her various roles and a sense for the process of supervision from engagement through the work phase. At the same time, she felt somewhat overwhelmed by the sheer volume of information she thought she needed to know, as well as the range of skills she believed necessary in order to do a good job. "I barely know enough to do my own clinical work well, no less supervise the clinical work of others," she said.

It takes a certain kind of courage to assume the responsibility of being a clinical supervisor. The welfare of others often depends on what we do, and there *is* a lot to know in order to do the job well. It is not surprising, therefore, that supervisors (at all experience levels) worry at times that they don't know "enough." I know I do. What I tell myself (and what I told my new supervisee) is that there is no "enough." Similar to the process of learning to do good clinical work, learning to supervise well is a never ending process. There is no absolute arrival or perfect end point that signifies "I'm there." There is, however, the possibility for an extremely creative, gratifying (albeit sometimes frustrating) journey toward excellence. Happy trails.

R.I.C.

Appendix A

Multicultural Competencies in Supervision*

I. Being Aware of Your Own Cultural Values and Biases
  A. With respect to *attitudes and beliefs*, culturally competent supervisors:
    1. Believe cultural self-awareness and sensitivity to one's own cultural heritage are essential.
    2. Are aware of how their own cultural background and experiences have influenced their attitudes, values, and biases about the supervisory process.
    3. Are able to recognize the limits of their expertise in multicultural supervision.
    4. Recognize their sources of discomfort with differences that exist between themselves and supervisees in terms of race, ethnicity, culture, gender, and sexual orientation.
  B. With respect to *knowledge*, culturally competent supervisors:
    1. Have specific knowledge about how their own racial and cultural heritage affects their perception of assessment, diagnosis, and treatment of the client cases that they supervise.
    2. Possess knowledge and understanding about how oppression, racism, discrimination, and stereotyping affect them and their supervisees in their work.
    3. Possess knowledge about their social advocacy responsibility as supervisors.

---

*Reprinted from Haynes, Corey, and Moulton (2003), pp. 147–148.

C. With respect to *skills*, culturally competent supervisors:
1. Seek out education, training, and consultation to improve their supervisory work with diverse populations.
2. Participate in ongoing self-exploration as racial and cultural beings.

II. Understanding the Worldview of Clients and Supervisees

A. With respect to *attitudes and beliefs*, culturally competent supervisors:
1. Are aware of their negative and positive emotional reactions toward other racial and ethnic groups that may prove detrimental to the counseling and supervisory relationship.
2. Are aware of stereotypes and preconceived notions that they may hold toward diverse client and supervisee populations.

B. With respect to *knowledge*, culturally competent supervisors:
1. Possess specific knowledge and information about the supervisees and clients for which they are responsible.
2. Understand how race, culture, ethnicity, age, religion, gender, and sexual orientation influence the ways supervisees and clients function in the world.
3. Understand and have knowledge about how sociopolitical factors affect the personal development of supervisees and the clients they serve.

C. With respect to *skills*, culturally competent supervisors:
1. Have a working knowledge and train their supervisees about mental health and mental disorders that affect various ethnic and racial groups.
2. Interact with diverse populations professionally and in the communities they serve.

III. Developing Culturally Appropriate Intervention Strategies and Techniques

A. With respect to *attitudes and beliefs*, culturally competent supervisors:
1. Model respect for supervisees' and clients' religious and spiritual beliefs and values.
2. Respect the needs of diverse populations in selecting intervention strategies that are appropriate for specific cultures.

B. With respect to *knowledge*, culturally competent supervisors:
1. Have a clear and explicit knowledge and understanding of the models and methods of counseling and supervision and the degree to which they fit with the values of diverse groups.
2. Are aware of barriers that prevent diverse populations from accessing mental health care.
3. Have knowledge of the potential cultural bias in assessment, diagnosis, treatment, and evaluation.
4. Have knowledge of family and community systems of the diverse populations they serve.
5. Are aware of relevant discriminatory practices at the professional and the community level of the supervisees and clients they serve.

C. With respect to *skills*, culturally competent supervisors:
   1. Use a variety of supervision methods that are congruent with the diverse backgrounds of supervisees.
   2. Use relationship skills consistent with the cultural background of supervisees and their clients.
   3. Are responsible to train supervisees in multicultural case conceptualization as it pertains to assessment, diagnosis, and treatment.
   4. Are able to help supervisees assist their clients in determining whether a problem stems from racism or bias so that clients do not inappropriately personalize problems.
   5. Are open to seek consultation for alternative treatment strategies to meet the needs of the diverse populations they serve.
   6. Can teach their supervisees about potential bias and the appropriate use of traditional assessment and testing instruments when working with diverse populations.
   7. Assist supervisees in reducing or eliminating biases, prejudices, and discriminatory practices as they pertain to diverse groups.
   8. Take responsibility for educating their supervisees through the use of a supervision contract that includes multicultural dimensions of supervision.

Appendix B[†]

The Multicultural Awareness, Knowledge, and Skills Survey (MAKSS)*

MULTICULTURAL AWARENESS

1. One of the potential negative consequences about gaining information concerning specific cultures is that students might stereotype members of those cultural groups according to the information they have gained.

   Strongly disagree   Disagree   Agree   Strongly agree

2. At this time in your life, how would you rate yourself in terms of understanding how your cultural background has influenced the way you think and act?

   Very limited   Limited   Fairly aware   Very aware

3. At this point in your life, how would you rate your understanding of the impact of the way you think and act when interacting with persons of different cultural backgrounds?

   Very limited   Limited   Fairly aware   Very aware

†From Covey/Covey, *Groups: Process and Practice,* Sixth Edition. Brooks/Cole, Pacific Grove, CA. Used with permission.

*The MAKSS has been developed by Michael D'Andrea, Ed.D., Judy Daniels, Ed.D., and Ronald Heck, Ph.D., Department of Counselor Education, University of Hawaii, Manoa, 1776 University Ave., WA2-221, Honolulu, Hawaii 96822: (808) 956-7904. Used by permission.

4. The human service professions, especially counseling and clinical psychology, have failed to meet the mental health needs of ethnic minorities.

   Strongly disagree   Disagree   (Agree)   Strongly agree

5. At the present time, how would you generally rate yourself in terms of being able to accurately compare your own cultural perspective with that of a person from another culture?

   Very limited   Limited   (Good)   Very good

6. The criteria of self-awareness, self-fulfillment, and self-discovery are important measures in most counseling sessions.

   Strongly disagree   Disagree   (Agree)   Strongly agree

7. Promoting a client's sense of psychological independence is usually a safe goal to strive for in most counseling situations.

   Strongly disagree   (Disagree)   Agree   Strongly agree

8. How would you react to the following statement? In general, counseling services should be directed toward assisting clients to adjust to stressful environmental situations.

   Strongly disagree   (Disagree)   Agree   Strongly agree

9. Psychological problems vary with the culture of the client.

   Strongly disagree   (Disagree)   Agree   Strongly agree

10. There are some basic counseling skills that are applicable to create successful outcomes regardless of the client's cultural background.

    Strongly disagree   Disagree   (Agree)   Strongly agree

MULTICULTURAL KNOWLEDGE

At the present time, how would you rate your own understanding of the following terms:

11. Culture

    Very limited   Limited   (Good)   Very good

12. Ethnicity

    Very limited   Limited   (Good)   Very good

13. Racism

    Very limited   Limited   (Good)   Very good

14. Prejudice

Very limited   Limited   Good   Very good

15. Multicultural Counseling

Very limited   Limited   Good   Very good

16. Ethnocentrism

Very limited   Limited   Good   Very good

17. Cultural Encapsulation

Very limited   Limited   Good   Very good

18. In counseling, clients from different ethnic/cultural backgrounds should be given the same treatment that White mainstream clients receive.

Strongly disagree   Disagree   Agree   Strongly agree

19. The difficulty with the concept of "integration" is its implicit bias in favor of the dominant culture.

Strongly disagree   Disagree   Agree   Strongly agree

20. Racial and ethnic persons are underrepresented in clinical and counseling psychology.

Strongly disagree   Disagree   Agree   Strongly agree

MULTICULTURAL SKILLS

21. How would you rate your ability to conduct an effective counseling interview with a person from a cultural background significantly different from your own?

Very limited   Limited   Good   Very good

22. How would you rate your ability to effectively assess the mental health needs of a person from a cultural background significantly different from your own?

Very limited   Limited   Good   Very good

23. In general, how would you rate yourself in terms of being able to effectively deal with biases, discrimination, and prejudices directed at you by a client in a counseling setting?

Very limited   Limited   Good   Very good

24. How well would you rate your ability to accurately identify culturally biased assumptions as they relate to your professional training?

Very limited   Limited   Good   Very good

25. In general, how would you rate your skill level in terms of being able to provide appropriate counseling services to culturally different clients?

    Very limited   Limited   Good   Very good

26. How would you rate your ability to effectively secure information and resources to better serve culturally different clients?

    Very limited   Limited   Good   Very good

27. How would you rate your ability to accurately assess the mental health needs of women?

    Very limited   Limited   Good   Very good

28. How would you rate your ability to accurately assess the mental health needs of men?

    Very limited   Limited   Good   Very good

29. How well would you rate your ability to accurately assess the mental health needs of older adults?

    Very limited   Limited   Good   Very good

30. How well would you rate your ability to accurately assess the mental health needs of persons who come from very poor socioeconomic backgrounds?

    Very limited   Limited   Good   Very good

Appendix C

Educational Assessment Scale (EAS)

DR. CARLTON E. MUNSON

The following questions are to help your supervisor plan your supervisory learning needs. There are no correct or incorrect answers. Answer the questions factually. The objective is to be able to assess what you presently know and what areas need development. It is expected that there will be a number of areas in which you will have limited or no knowledge. Do not feel bad that you have limited knowledge in a given area. This instrument will be helpful only if you identify accurately what you know and do not know.

1. *Previous Experience*

    Total years social work paid experience: _____
    List job responsibilities:

    Total years volunteer social work experience: _____
    List job responsibilities:

    Total years non-social work experience: _____
    List job responsibilities:

From Carlton E. Munson (2002). *Handbook of Clinical Social Work Supervision*. New York: Haworth Social Work Practice Press, pp. 498–502.

2. *Ethical Awareness*

Have you read the social work code of ethics?   □No   □Yes

If yes, how many years has it been since you read the code of ethics? _____

Have you taken the Munson Code of Ethics Scale?   □No   □Yes

If yes, give your score: _____
and the date taken: _____

Circle the number to the right in each area to indicate your level of knowledge or ability.

3. *Theoretical Knowledge*

	None	Little	Some		Moderate		Strong		Thorough	
Psychoanalytic	1	2	3	4	5	6	7	8	9	10
Adlerian	1	2	3	4	5	6	7	8	9	10
Jungian	1	2	3	4	5	6	7	8	9	10
Person-centered	1	2	3	4	5	6	7	8	9	10
Rational-emotive	1	2	3	4	5	6	7	8	9	10
Behavioral	1	2	3	4	5	6	7	8	9	10
Gestalt	1	2	3	4	5	6	7	8	9	10
Reality therapy	1	2	3	4	5	6	7	8	9	10
Existential	1	2	3	4	5	6	7	8	9	10
Transactional	1	2	3	4	5	6	7	8	9	10
Analysis	1	2	3	4	5	6	7	8	9	10
Psychodrama	1	2	3	4	5	6	7	8	9	10
Family therapy	1	2	3	4	5	6	7	8	9	10
Human potential	1	2	3	4	5	6	7	8	9	10
Communication	1	2	3	4	5	6	7	8	9	10

Indicate theories not listed above that you have utilized or know. Use the number scale to indicate your knowledge level for each theory listed:

4. *Assessment and Diagnosis*

	None	Some	Average	Extensive	Thorough
Social assessment	1	2	3	4	5
Use of DSM-IV-TR	1	2	3	4	5
Initial database	1	2	3	4	5
Initial treatment plans	1	2	3	4	5
Review treatment plans	1	2	3	4	5
Evaluating mental status	1	2	3	4	5
Interview evaluation	1	2	3	4	5
Social assessment	1	2	3	4	5
Psychological assessment	1	2	3	4	5

5. *Intervention*

	None	Some	Average	Extensive	Thorough
Forming alliances	1	2	3	4	5
Client engagement	1	2	3	4	5
Client confusion	1	2	3	4	5
Client hostility	1	2	3	4	5
Client resistance	1	2	3	4	5
Interpretations	1	2	3	4	5
Seeking clarification	1	2	3	4	5
Being supportive	1	2	3	4	5
Asking sensitive questions	1	2	3	4	5
Transference	1	2	3	4	5
Countertransference	1	2	3	4	5
Termination	1	2	3	4	5

6. *Record Keeping*

	None	Some	Average	Extensive	Thorough
Initial databases	1	2	3	4	5
Initial treatment plans	1	2	3	4	5
Review treatment plans	1	2	3	4	5
Progress notes	1	2	3	4	5
Invoicing	1	2	3	4	5
Outcome measures	1	2	3	4	5
Case management	1	2	3	4	5

7. *Prior Supervisory Experience*

List your past supervisory experiences. Include supervision of all types of past employment. Include in the listing your likes and dislikes in each supervisory experience.

8. *Strengths and Limitations*

Identify personal and professional strengths and limitations that could enhance or hinder your practice activity and performance in supervision.

9. *View of Helping*

What are your views and attitudes about clients and the helping relationship?

10. *Goals*

List your learning goals in supervision:

List your career goals and objectives:

What do you see as the relationship between your current learning goals and your career objectives?

Appendix D

A Blueprint for Developmental Supervision*

1. **Beginning Stage:** The goal of this stage is to develop the relationship, assess competencies, educate, and monitor early experiences.

Supervisor

Assume primary responsibility and encourage supervisee

Assess supervisee's strengths and weaknesses in areas of training, experience, and clinical competence (assessment, direct treatment, and interpersonal style)

Use supervisee assessment information to develop goals with the supervisee

Review and sign supervisory contract and other supervisory agreements

Critically review each of the supervisee's prospective clients for appropriate placement

Supervisee

Seek and accept direction

Discuss perception of strengths and weaknesses with supervisor

Provide supervisor with information requested

Review and sign contract and supervisory agreements

Set supervision goals in collaboration with supervisor

Practice safe and prudent therapy within the structure provided by supervisor

Review policies and procedures for practice and seek clarification

*From Haynes, R., Corey, G., and Moulton, P., *Clinical Supervision in the Helping Professions.* Brooks/Cole, Pacific Grove, CA. Used with permission.

Set supervisory goals collaboratively with supervisee

Review policies and procedures of practice (address ethics, confidentiality, and emergency procedures)

Educate supervisee in areas of need to include ethics, liability, assessment, organization of information, documentation, and therapeutic skills

Provide direct and consistent observation of therapy (live supervision, video, one-way mirror, bug-in-the-ear)

Provide structure for supervisory sessions

Limit autonomy until competence in performance is evidenced

Provide direct feedback often and combine with information and practice as needed

Be available for direct intervention in critical incidents (with supervisee and clients)

Review and approve all documentation (assist in writing if needed)

Document supervisory activities

Be willing to take risks and practice within the boundaries of the supervisory relationship

Question and hypothesize

Provide information to supervisor regarding wants and expectations of supervision

Recognize that anxiety is normal and discuss concerns with supervisor

2. **Middle Stage:** The goal of this stage is to transition from dependency to independent practice. This stage is often characterized by a struggle in the supervisory relationship as supervisees want to move forward and supervisors want to tread carefully.

Supervisor
Role-play, provide ethical dilemmas, play devil's advocate, and design "what if" scenarios for supervisee to explore and discuss

Suggest various theoretical approaches for each given case

Facilitate discussion of various treatment alternatives

Assist supervisee in choosing a sound course of action

Supervisee
Practice presenting cases in a professional manner

Explore theoretical orientation with supervisor

Actively participate an identification of treatment techniques and strategies

Consult with supervisor for direction

Initiate interventions independently

Provide information to supervisor to assure client welfare

Provide supervisee with opportunities to discuss client and presenting problems from supervisee's perspective

Share responsibility with supervisee

Monitor by direct observation, documentation review, and self-report

Create opportunities for supervisee to struggle with decisions and consequences

Ask questions and expect supervisee to seek answers (be prepared to assist)

Serve as a resource and reference for materials, problem solving, and practice

Encourage supervisee to present cases in a collaborative manner

Collaboratively make decisions about how much time to spend on each case

Share responsibility for the supervision session structure

Reduce directive stance and encourage democratic decision making

Provide formative feedback consistently, and develop a plan of action collaboratively with supervisee for improvement

Document supervisory practice

Choose approach for case conceptualization and share with supervisor

Identify relevant questions and strategies for gaining information

Draft reports and explain formulation and process to supervisor

Assume comprehensive case management duties

Share responsibility with supervisor for client care

Share responsibility for structure of supervisory sessions

Come to supervision sessions prepared to initiate topics for discussion

Provide feedback to supervisor on the supervision received and identify and voice perceptions of unmet needs

3. **Ending Stage:** The primary goal of this stage is to foster independence and prepare supervisee for work as an independent professional.

Supervisor
Review goals and progress

Listen to and encourage supervisee

Monitor primarily through self-report and documentation with occasional direct observation

Supervisee
Articulate theoretical orientation, treatment alternatives explored, and course of action chosen

Provide justification for any given course of action in treatment

Provide summative evaluation

Take responsibility for termination of formal supervisory relationship

Document supervisory process

Acknowledge continued vicarious and direct liability throughout the supervisory relationship

Be open to and seek evaluative feedback on the supervisory process, the structure of supervision, and specific supervisory skills

Recognize and identify skills for future development

Assume primary responsibility for client welfare

Review goals and progress

Review learning during supervision

Determine future goals and course of action

Think out loud while problem solving and conceptualizing client information

Increase independent decision making

Be self-supervising

Reflect on the supervisory process and provide supervisor with evaluative feedback

References

Anderson, J. (1997). *Social work with groups: A process model*. Reading, MA: Addison-Wesley.

Anderson, T. (1987). The reflecting team: Dialogue and meta-dialogue in clinical work. *Family Process, 26*, 415–428.

Barrett-Lennard, G. T. (1981). The empathy cycle: Refinement of a nuclear concept. *Journal of Counseling Psychology, 28*, 91–100.

Bernard, J., & Goodyear, R. (1998). *Fundamentals of clinical supervision* (2nd ed.). Boston: Allyn & Bacon.

Carkhuff, R. R., & Anthony, W. A. (1979). *The skills of helping: An introduction to counseling*. Amherst, MA: Human Resource Development Press.

Cournoyer, B. (1991). *The social work skills workbook*. Belmont, CA: Wadsworth.

Covey, S. (1989). *The seven habits of highly effective people: Restoring the character ethic*. New York: Simon & Schuster.

Covey, M., & Covey, G. (2002). *Groups: Process and practice* (6th ed.). Pacific Grove, CA: Brooks/Cole.

D'Andrea, M., Daniels, J., & Heck, R. (1991). *The multicultural awareness, knowledge, and skills survey (MAKKS)*. Honolulu, HI: University of Hawaii.

De Jong, P., & Berg, I. K. (2002). *Interviewing for solutions* (2nd ed.). Pacific Grove, CA: Brooks/Cole.

De Jong, P., & Miller, S. D. (1995). How to interview for client strengths. *Social Work, 40*, 729–736.

De Shazer, S. (1985). *Keys to solution in brief therapy*. New York: Norton.

Duan, C., & Hill, C. E. (1996). The current state of empathy research. *Journal of Counseling Psychology, 43*, 261–274.

Eckstein, R., & Wallerstein, R. (1958). *The teaching and learning of psychotherapy*. New York: Basic Books.

Edwards, J. K., & Chen, M. (1999). Strength based supervision: Frameworks, current practice, and future directions: A Wu-wei method. *Family Journal, 7*, 349–357.

Egan, G. (2002). *The skilled helper: A problem-management and opportunity-development approach to helping* (7th ed.). Pacific Grove, CA: Brooks/Cole.

Ellis, A. (1962). *Reason and emotion in psychotherapy.* Hollywood, CA: Wilshire.

Evans, D., Hearn, M. T., Uhlemann, M., & Ivey, A. (1989). *Essential interviewing: A programmed approach to effective communication* (3rd ed.). Pacific Grove, CA: Brooks/Cole.

Falvey, J. E. (2002). *Managing clinical supervision: Ethical practice and legal risk management.* Pacific Grove, CA: Brooks/Cole.

Fischer, J. (1978). *Effective casework practice: An eclectic approach.* New York: McGraw-Hill.

Fisher, R., & Ury, W. (1991). *Getting to yes: Negotiating agreement without giving in.* New York: Penguin Books.

Fong, R. (2001). Culturally competent social work practice: Past and present. In R. Fong & S. Furuto (Eds.), *Culturally competent practice: Skills, interventions, and evaluations* (pp. 1–9). Boston: Allyn & Bacon.

Fong, R., Boyd, T., & Browne, C. (1999). The Gandhi Technique: A biculturalization approach for empowering Asian and Pacific Islander families. *Journal of Multicultural Social Work, 7,* 95–110.

Goldfried, M. R., & Davison, G. C. (1976). *Clinical behavior therapy.* New York: Holt, Rinehart and Winston.

Gudykunst, W. B. (1991). *Bridging differences: Effective intergroup communication.* Newbury Park, CA: Sage.

Hargrove, R. A. (2000). *Masterful coaching fieldbook.* San Francisco, CA: Jossey-Bass/Pfeiffer.

Haynes, R., Corey, G., & Moulton, P. (2003). *Clinical supervision in the helping professions.* Pacific Grove, CA: Brooks/Cole.

Hersey, P., & Blanchard, K. (1982). *Management of organizational behavior: Utilizing human resources.* Englewood Cliffs, NJ: Prentice Hall.

Holloway, E. (1995). *Clinical supervision: A systems approach.* Thousand Oaks, CA: Sage.

Ivey, A. E. (1971). *Microcounseling.* Springfield, IL: Charles C. Thomas.

Ivey, A. E., & Authier, J. (1978). *Microcounseling: Innovations in interviewing training.* Springfield, IL: Charles C. Thomas.

Ivey, A., & Ivey, M. B. (1999). *Intentional interviewing and counseling: Facilitating client development in a multicultural society* (4th ed.). Pacific Grove, CA: Brooks/Cole.

Kadushin, A., & Harkness, D. (2002). *Supervision in social work* (4th ed.). New York: Columbia University Press.

Kagan, H. K., & Kagan, N. I. (1997). Interpersonal process recall: Influencing human interaction. In C. E. Watkins, Jr. (Ed.), *Handbook of psychotherapy supervision* (pp. 296–309). New York: Wiley.

Kaiser, T. (1997). *Supervisory relationships: Exploring the human element.* Pacific Grove, CA: Brooks/Cole.

Knowles, M. S., Holton, E. F., & Swanson, R. A. (1998). *The adult learner* (5th ed.). Woburn, MA: Butterworth-Heinemann.

Kolb, D. A. (1976). *The learning styles inventory: Technical manual.* Boston: Mcber.

Kolb, D. A. (1984). *Experiential learning: Experience as the source of learning and development.* Englewood Cliffs, NJ: Prentice Hall.

Kraines, G. (1991). Stress in the workplace. *Directions in Psychiatry, 11,* 30–37.

Levy, C. S. (1993). The value base of social work. *Journal of Education for Social Work, 9,* 34–42.

Lum, D. (1999). *Culturally competent practice: A framework for growth and action.* Pacific Grove, CA: Brooks/Cole.

Lum, D. (2000). *Social work practice and people of color: A process-stage approach* (4th ed.). Belmont, CA: Brooks/Cole.

McCollum, E., & Wetchler, J. (1995). In defense of case consultation: Maybe "dead" supervision isn't dead after all. *Journal of Marital and Family Therapy, 21,* 155–166.

Meichenbaum, D. H., & Cameron, R. (1974). The clinical potential of modifying what clients say to themselves. In M. J. Mahoney & C. E. Thoresen (Eds.), *Self-control: Power to the person.* Monterey, CA: Brooks-Cole.

Munson, C. (2002). *Handbook of clinical social work supervision* (3rd ed.). New York: Haworth.

Murphy, B. C., & Dillon, C. (1998). *Interviewing in action: Process and practice.* Pacific Grove, CA: Brooks/Cole.

Myers, I. B. (1962). *The Myers-Briggs Type Indicator.* Palo Alto, CA: Consulting Psychologists Press.

Myers, I. B., & McCaulley, M. H. (1985). *Manual: A guide to the development and use of the Myers-Briggs Type Indicator.* Palo Alto, CA: Consulting Psychologists Press.

Negotiation Training [Training Manual]. (2001). Narragansett, RI: Management Support Services.

Noddings, N. (1984). *Caring: A feminine approach to ethics and moral education.* Berkeley, CA: University of California Press.

Reamer, F. G. (1995). *Social work values and ethics.* New York: Columbia University Press.

Reamer, F. G. (2003). *Social work malpractice and liability* (2nd ed.). New York: Columbia University Press.

Robiner, W. N., Fuhrman, M. J., & Bobbitt, B. L. (1990). Supervision in the practice of psychology: Toward the development of a supervisory instrument. *Psychotherapy in Private Practice, 8,* 87–98.

Robinar, W. N., Fuhrman, M. J., & Risvedt, S. (1993). Evaluation difficulties in supervising psychology interns. *Clinical Psychologist, 46,* 3–13.

Rogers, C. (1975). Empathy: An unappreciated way of being. *Counseling Psychologist, 21,* 95–103.

Saleebey, D. (1992). Introduction: Power in the people. In D. Saleebey (Ed.), *The strengths perspective in social work practice.* New York: Longman.

Shulman, L. (1993). *Interactional supervision.* Washington, DC: National Association of Social Workers.

Stahl, M. J. (1995). *Management: Total quality in a global environment.* Cambridge, MA: Blackwell.

Tarasoff v. Regents of the University of California, 551 P.2d 334 (Cal. 1976).

White, M., & Epston, D. (1990). *Narrative means to therapeutic ends.* Adelaide, South Australia: Dulwich Centre.

Yalom, I. D. (1995). *The theory and practice of group psychotherapy* (4th ed.). New York: Basic Books.

Zander, R. S., & Zander, B. (2000). *The art of possibility.* Boston: Harvard Business School Press.

Index

TO THE OWNER OF THIS BOOK:

I hope that you have found *Clinical Supervision: What to Do and How to Do It* useful. So that this book can be improved in a future edition, would you take the time to complete this sheet and return it? Thank you.

School and address: _____

_____

Department: _____

Instructor's name: _____

1. What I like most about this book is: _____

_____

_____

2. What I like least about this book is: _____

_____

_____

3. My general reaction to this book is: _____

_____

_____

4. The name of the course in which I used this book is: _____

_____

5. Were all of the chapters of the book assigned for you to read?_____

   If not, which ones weren't? _____

6. In the space below, or on a separate sheet of paper, please write specific suggestions for improving this book and anything else you'd care to share about your experience in using this book.

_____

_____

_____

_____

OPTIONAL:

Your name: _____ Date: _____

May we quote you, either in promotion for *Clinical Supervision: What to Do and How to Do It,* or in future publishing ventures?

    Yes: _____ No: _____

    Sincerely yours,

    Robert I. Cohen

FOLD HERE